THE PERFORMANCE ASSESSMENT HANDBOOK

VOLUME 1
PORTFOLIOS AND SOCRATIC SEMINARS

Designs from the Field and Guidelines for the Territory Ahead

Bil Johnson

EYE ON EDUCATION

EYE ON EDUCATION
P.O. BOX 3113
PRINCETON, N.J. 08543
(609) 395-0005
(609) 395-1180 fax

Editorial and production services provided by Richard H. Adin Freelance Editorial
Services, 9 Orchard Drive, Gardiner, NY 12525 (914-883-5884)

For information about permission to reproduce selections from this book, write:
Eye On Education, Permissions Dept., P.O. Box 3113, Princeton, NJ 08543

ISBN 1-883001-16-1

Library of Congress Cataloging-in-Publication Data

Johnson, Bil, 1949–
        The performance assessment handbook : designs from the field
    and guidelines for the territory ahead / Bil Johnson
                p.   cm.
    Includes bibliographical references.
    ISBN 1-883001-16-1 (v. 1). — ISBN 1-883001-17-X (v. 2)
    1. Educational tests and measurements — United States — Handbooks,
manuals, etc. 2. Portfolios in education — United States — Handbooks,
manuals, etc. 3. Competency based educational tests — United States —
Handbooks, manuals, etc. I. Title.
LB3051.J566 1996
371.2'6 — dc20   95-39968
                                                            CIP

10 9 8 7 6 5 4 3

If you like this book, we recommend:

THE PERFORMANCE ASSESSMENT HANDBOOK
VOLUME 2: PERFORMANCES AND EXHIBITIONS
Designs from the Field and Guidelines for the Territory Ahead
by Bil Johnson

Also Available from Eye On Education:

THE LIBRARY OF INNOVATIONS

Educational Technology: Best Practices from America's Schools
by William C. Bozeman and Donna J. Baumbach

Block Scheduling: A Catalyst for Change in High Schools
by Robert Lynn Canady and Michael D. Rettig

Innovations in Parent and Family Involvement
by William Rioux and Nancy Berla

The Directory of Innovations in High Schools
by Gloria G. Frazier and Robert N. Sickles

Research on Educational Innovations
by Arthur K. Ellis and Jeffrey T. Fouts

Research on School Restructuring
by Arthur K. Ellis and Jeffrey T. Fouts

THE LEADERSHIP AND MANAGEMENT SERIES

The Principal's Edge
by Jack McCall

Hands-on Leadership Tools for Principals
by Ray Calabrese, Gary Short, and Sally Zepeda

Quality and Education: Critical Linkages
by Betty L. McCormick

Transforming Education Through Total Quality Management: A Practitioner's Guide
by Franklin P. Schargel

The Educator's Guide to Implementing Outcomes
by William J. Smith

The School Portfolio: A Comprehensive Framework for School Improvement
by Victoria L. Bernhardt

Schools for All Learners: Beyond the Bell Curve
by Renfro C. Manning

The Administrator's Guide to School-Community Relations
by George E. Pawlas

Dedication

To my mother, for her energy and intellect;
To my father, who taught me about teaching;
To my brother, who taught me about learning.

ABOUT THE AUTHOR

Bil Johnson is a member of the National Re: Learning Faculty of the Annenberg Institute for School Reform. He has taught secondary English and Social Studies in the public schools since 1971. Johnson has been an active member of the Coalition of Essential Schools for 10 years, and is currently Lead Teacher at the Francis W. Parker Charter School in Fort Devens, Massachusetts.

TABLE OF CONTENTS

ACKNOWLEDGMENTS

More than most, this book really *does* owe a huge amount to other people. Because it is composed of examples *from the field*, I am indebted to all the teachers who contributed the work which made this possible. Their efforts in performance assessment are leading the way into new frontiers in teaching and learning. I only hope these volumes do justice to their efforts.

Numerous others supported my work throughout the writing of this book and in the years leading up to it when I was exploring the use of new assessments. I have to particularly thank Grant Wiggins for his encouragement, honesty, and inspiration over the years. Likewise, the support and positive feedback from Heidi Hayes Jacobs helped shape many of the ideas which appear here.

There are too many people at the Coalition of Essential Schools to thank them all, but those who have had the patience and energy to always find time to listen and critique my work deserve mention. Paula Evans, Gene Thompson-Grove, Joe McDonald, Kitty Pucci, Kathy DiNitto, Pat Wasley, and Ted Sizer have been among that number. Colleagues with the National Re:Learning Faculty at the Coalition who have contributed ideas and support include Michael Patron, Carol Lacerenza-Bjork, Cheri Dedmon, Jude Pelchat, Dot Turner, and Steve Cantrell.

The Four Seasons Project at Teachers College, Columbia University, under the umbrella of the National Center for Restructuring Education, Schools, and Teaching, has provided me with another set of colleagues whose examples proliferate this book, as do many of their valuable ideas. Joel Kammer, Linda Quinn, Carol Coe, Linda Caldwell Dancy, Betty Kreitzer, Gary Obermeyer, Judy Onufer, Lynn Beebe, Millie Sanders, Jerry Howland, Rick Casey, Jan Hoff, and many other Four Seasons Faculty are among the finest teachers I have had the pleasure to work with over the years. Among the staff at NCREST, Linda Darling-Hammond, Ann Lieberman, Maritza McDonald, David Zuckerman, Kathe Jervis, Susan London, Rob

Southworth, and Terry Baker have all had a hand in shaping the work presented here.

I need to thank those friends in New York and Boston who have put up with eccentricities, idiosyncrasies, and general careening. In New York, Ilene Kristen, Ahvi Spindell, Jane Gabbert, Mandy Gersten, Anthony Angotta, John Chambers, Maureen Grolnick, Sherry King, Laura Lipton, Phil Kuczma, and Jay Fasold all had to listen to these ideas for years and years. In Boston, I received great support from Kathleen Cushman, Jamie Jacobs, Patti Jacobs, Charlie Berg, and Craig Lambert. I sincerely thank each of them.

Finally, I'd like to thank Bob Sickles, the publisher of this book, for his support and encouragement, his patience and guidance, and for believing in books like this. He is building a valuable library for educators of all levels.

Bil Johnson
Cambridge, MA
October 7, 1995

AUTHOR'S NOTE

The Author would like to thank the following educators who have made contributions to this volume and have generously granted permission to include their materials:

Heathwood Hall Episcopal School
Columbia, South Carolina
    D. Venable, A. Haviland, A. Venable, C. Haigler

The Crefeld School
Philadelphia, Pennsylvania
    Michael Patron, Headmaster, and Staff

Central Park East Secondary School
New York, New York
    Paul Schwarz and David Smith, Codirectors and Staff

Academy for the Middle Years – Northwest
Philadelphia, Pennsylvania
    Gert Kline and Janet Malloy

Fulton Valley Prep, Piner High School
Santa Rosa, California
    Kathy Juarez, Humanities Team, and Science Staff

Garden City High School
Garden City, New York
    Carlo Rebolini

Brookline High School
Brookline, Massachusetts
    Margaret Metzger

Bronxville High School
Bronxville, New York
    Linda Passman and Mary Schenck

Pierre Van Cortlandt Middle School
Croton-on-Hudson, New York
    Rick Casey

FOREWORD

While America's educational leaders have long been devotees of testing, the current decade has unleashed a veritable flood of interest in and application of "assessment." The current prime question "Does it work?" arises both from a feeling of dismay about the quality of American schools and a stance of high distrust of the teachers and administrators who make up the system of these schools. Some of this testing craze is an affront, both to professionals and to scholars, who know full well the limitations of existing assessment "instruments" (the word itself says worlds).

What Bil Johnson has done in these two volumes is not so much to curse the darkness as to light some candles — turning assessment on its head by seeing it as a way to enliven and redirect teaching. Asking good "test" questions is simply asking good questions, the stock and trade of fine teachers and classrooms. The Socratic seminar not only goes back many centuries but both energizes the understanding of students and provides teachers with some sense of how those students' minds work. Johnson, a veteran teacher and scholar, has given us here a rich array of examples of the interwoven worlds of good teaching and reasonable assessment.

Throughout these books, Johnson's absolute trust in classroom teachers is powerfully implicit. Teachers will make a difference, not tests or the carrots and sticks which political leaders might attach to the results of those tests. Only teachers can both serve students in helping them to use their minds well and at the same time plumb those same students' work in a way that informs both students and structures, all the while presenting evidence of the larger world of where each students is and of whether his or her school "works."

These are books of helpful provocations. Those of us who teach will be stimulated by them, stimulated as Johnson would have us stimulate our students.

Theodore R. Sizer

1

THE TERRITORY AHEAD
PERFORMANCE ASSESSMENTS
AND THE
TERRITORY AHEAD

This is a book for teachers — particularly secondary school teachers. It is about an area within their immediate domain and requires their thoughtful, reflective, and energetic commitment. If teachers and students are not the central players in the performance assessment reforms which occur in our schools, there is probably no chance for that movement's success.

Performance assessment is *not* something which can be "learned" at a one-shot, "In-Service Day" inoculation — after which too many administrators and department heads charge their staff with implementation by Monday! Performance assessment *programs* must become part of a larger, ongoing professional development initiative which is designed to reshape the school as a learning community. This is a radical departure from what presently exists. This means reassessing the assumptions and goals of every member of the present community — from school boards, to parents, to teachers, to unions, to administrators, to students.

There are numerous books about those school redesign and restructuring possibilities (*see* Sizer, Schlecty, et al.). This book is about the practical steps teachers can begin, *with their students*, to reculture their classrooms and their schools — not an easy row to hoe. It requires hard work, making mistakes, taking risks, arguing with friends, second-guessing yourself, and a host of other problems.

1

But it is aimed at keeping high quality student work *central* — a goal few schools remain true to at present — and it is designed to genuinely *empower* teachers to lead the way.

What should those students know and be able to do? How will teachers, parents, community *really know* what students have learned? In what ways will we assess their programs? Will we establish graduation systems which require performance and exhibition of student knowledge and ability and not just be certification of school attendance? These are the questions *The Performance Assessment Handbook* addresses.

This book provides examples of work teachers are doing with their students *right now*. These are the pioneers in the *territory ahead*. The trails they are blazing are seldom straight and clean; some are deadends, while others terminate at a chasm or precipice. Yet they persist. And their students respond, joining them in this a new adventure. There is a vitality which Performance Assessments bring with them that is hard to describe because it doesn't fit the current paradigms of school. Classrooms are "busy" and noisy, students have a voice and have choices; teachers model risk-taking and lifelong learning behaviors, sharing their curiosity, questions, and confusion with their students. Parents are invited to join the process, to understand the goals of the journey, to support the teachers and students in their desire to find better ways to assess *genuine student progress* and more clearly define quality work.

These are complex and difficult tasks, still in their research and development phase. Meaningful *change* does not come quickly or without struggle. Think about anyone's personal journey through adolescence, during which time we experience the most extreme personal, intellectual, psychological, social, and emotional changes in our growth. This does not happen quickly (could it *ever* happen quickly enough for a teenager?) and it does not happen without struggle, pain, agony, and ecstasy. The kind of change *Performance Assessment* introduces to teachers and students, parents and community, school boards and administrators, is equally radical. It will not happen overnight and it will not happen without mistakes, retrenchment, two-steps-forward-and-one-step-back. And it *cannot* happen without things looking very different by the time the journey ends. Compare photos of the same person at ages 12 and 21 — how radical are the changes in looks, dress, attitude?

What is being asked of teachers and schools, when they commit to implementing a performance assessment system, is a radical change similar to that of an adolescent. It will take years; you will mature; you will know far more at the end of the time than you knew at the beginning, but you *had to* learn some things the hard way. You will still need to learn a lot, and grow more, in new ways — but you will be far better prepared to do that.

Dennie Wolf of Harvard has referred to the performance assessment movement as "the flying wedge of school reform" and I agree with her. Because the examination of assessment cannot be separated from scrutinizing curriculum and instruction, assessment opens a can of worms which includes not only curriculum and instruction but also some very basic concepts about integrating curriculum, scheduling, student voice, teacher-administrator relations, community activity, and standards, to name a few. Books could be written about *each* of these issues. Some already have been and we will undoubtedly see more. But the focus of this text is on assessment. The other issues cannot be avoided because assessment touches upon every aspect of schooling and is therefore a powerful factor in school reform and restructuring. The purpose here, however, is not to look comprehensively at reform and restructuring; rather, it is to examine assessment in a practical way for classroom teachers.

Many of the examples here are from schools affiliated with the Coalition of Essential Schools. There are also a number from schools associated with the Four Seasons Project out of Teachers College, Columbia University's National Center for Restructuring Education, Schools, and Teaching. There is no intended bias and their appearance is the result of a simple practicality — for almost all of the past decade I have worked in and with the Coalition Schools, and for the past 4 years, I have been a member of the Four Seasons Project's Faculty on Performance Assessments. Because these two organizations have focused on performance assessment, I have been fortunate to work with many teachers who have been implementing new assessments. As a result of that affiliation, and the generosity of my colleagues in those organizations, their work comprises the majority of examples here. That does not mean that these new assessments are not being implemented everywhere else, all over this country. On the contrary, Performance Assessment innovations are occurring on all levels in all kinds of schools all over this nation.

The format for presenting teachers' work here is straightforward. Initially it investigates the idea of testing: what is in place and how it got there; what is being attempted in the way of change. Significant to that change is a different approach to the process of assessment, curriculum, and instruction. Again, there are serious implications for school restructuring which cannot be divorced from assessment issues, but the thrust of the first chapter is to set the context for developing performance assessments. The basic concept is that teachers utilize a system of *planning backwards from Outcomes*, and shift the age-old linear paradigm of curriculum-instruction-testing to a new, more fluid design based on Figure 1-1.

FIG. 1-1: PLANNING BACKWARDS

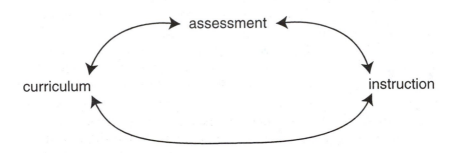

With that shift comes a movement away from teacher-centered, content-driven curriculum delivery, to a more student-centered, inquiry-driven curriculum. Such a shift *demands* new forms of assessment which are based on student *performance* of *knowledge-in-use*. A major shift for teachers, then, is conceiving of curriculum and instruction *integrated with* assessments, infusing the daily life of the classroom.

This book presents a wide variety of assessment approaches which teachers in many schools around the country are already using. The bulk of the text provides examples of work in either portfolio assessments and Socratic seminars (Vol. 1), or performance assessments and exhibitions (Vol. 2). Most significantly, *the teacher's voice* explains the development and use of the assessments presented here. The Outcomes, the Task Design, the Student Assignment, and the Results are also presented from the point of view of those teachers who executed the project. The purpose here is to provide the reader with a sense of how to develop assessments and to understand that performance assessments are always a *work in progress*. Even when assessments work well and students clearly achieve outcomes to high standards, teachers actively reflect on their work, looking to improve it for their next group. In some cases, we see a radical revision planned, in others, minor "fine-tuning." The fact that these assessments are part of a teaching/learning process *cannot be emphasized enough*. One of the key features related to changing the assessment systems in schools is the recognition that teaching and learning are an ongoing process which require constant reexamination, reflection, and revision.

A new assessment system also raises questions about standards, criteria, and rubrics. This is still a sticky area and one in which teachers and researchers need to begin more systematic work, establishing the reliability and validity of performance assessments. A chapter in Volume 2 is devoted to the questions and directions for research and data gathering those concepts raise.

Performance assessments raise the issue of standards and criteria in a manner which traditional testing has not. While performance assessments are definitely "messier" than straightforward, quantitative examinations which can be machine-scored, they truly push teachers, administrators, and community members to examine what it is we expect our students to show us they know and can do *in demonstrable ways*. By resisting the simplistic urge to reduce our students to a mere set of numbers, performance assessments force the adults of the learning community to examine what their real beliefs are regarding standards for excellent achievement. What is the level below which we will not award a diploma? Should it simply be a cut-off number or should it be a series of performance-based activities, requiring student engagement and activity to show more definitively what our students are capable of? Performance assessments require the latter of our students, therefore demanding that the adults clearly specify what those tasks, that engagement, and those demonstrations must consist of. Is it any wonder that people shy away from performance assessments shortly after they begin investigating them? This is hard work which requires deep and serious questioning about what we want from our schools and our students — in ways which we have not asked before. It is often easier to continue dancing with the devil we know, however inadequate, unfair, and unrevealing (regarding student knowledge and ability) that devil may be.

Nevertheless, there are teachers, schools, and communities, who are leading the way in this arena — developing and implementing new assessments, discussing and publishing their outcomes, preparing and presenting their students for public exhibitions. This book is a compilation of some of that work and a presentation of the ideas, arguments, and dilemmas that work evokes. The intent here is practical — this is a book primarily for teachers and students. The hope is that it will provoke thought, discussion, risk-taking, and, ultimately, the development of more effective assessments for students and teachers.

The Performance Assessment Handbook is a guidebook, a travelogue, a suggestion, a provocation, an invitation, a journal, and a question mark. It is designed to encourage, incite, prod, present, probe, upset, cheer, and share. The audience can be teachers, students, parents, school officials, or any other citizens who care about our students. The hope is that conversations will follow, attempts will be made, questions will be raised, and students will be better served.

In the mid-1990s America is an emerging nation again. The world is realigned, the population's demographics are radically shifting, technology is accelerating at ever faster rates. The America of the '50s and '60s is barely recognizable — but that can even be said for much of the '70s and '80s, too. Think about the technology in your life which didn't even exist 10–15 years ago. Consider, too, what the political and economic world was like then. And then consider that the students in our schools today were, at best, *just being born*.

Cable TV (MTV!), personal computers, the end of the Cold War, the first signs of international globalism (European Economic Community, NAFTA, etc.), the new waves of immigration to the United States — these are a quick list of the world *today's* student has been born into or is growing up in.

The education system was designed in 1893, for an emerging industrial society with an increasing southern and eastern European immigrant population — an age in which the factory was the dominant symbol. Can we still say that about 1995 or beyond?

Performance assessment systems are the new path described in *The Performance Assessment Handbook*. This book is designed to help explore the world of the 21st century, to prepare America's students to be ready for change, to adapt to new circumstances, to understand the shifting landscapes of a world which *can't* be anticipated. This book is simply designed to help people find where that path starts. Once there, the road is theirs to create. Like anything new, it's a little scary and a little exciting. Decide for yourself. Try it — even if it's just a few steps down the path. Maybe create your own trail. You'll meet some folks along the way — they're all through the following pages — and they'll try to help you keep moving forward. One warning, though: Everyone we know who has traveled into the *territory ahead*, the territory *The Performance Assessment Handbook* describes, has never come back. The good news is that they are doing quite well, thank you, and they haven't come back *by choice*. This volume gives you a chance to meet them and find out why they've continued to pioneer new paths — and invites you to join them.

2

SKYDIVING IN YOUR CLASSROOM: THE INDIVIDUAL AND REFORM

Early on in the second wave of school reform, shortly after *A Nation at Risk* was published in 1983, there was a popular notion that school reform concepts could be tested in classrooms or in "schools-within-schools" to determine their viability. The reasoning was that if some of these new reform ideas "worked," they would then be adopted by the larger school population, and school reform and restructuring would happen. The problem with this model, however, is that schools don't operate that way. The basic assumption is simply incorrect. Because of the insular nature of classroom

9

teaching, very little, in the way of innovation, ever flows from one room to another.

Research and development is an integral part of American industry. New product ideas are conceived, developed, tested and, if successful, produced and marketed. Schools-within-schools and classroom pioneers are education's version of the research and development concept. The problem, however, is that there is no mechanism to produce and market *anything* in public schools, other than the latest editions of textbooks. The culture of cellular activity and isolation is the dominant mode of schools. There is no example of successful classroom innovation, or a "successful" school-within-a-school model being adopted schoolwide or system-wide. Changes have occurred, particularly in areas like whole language and the writing process; but even in those instances, pockets of resistance remain. The American School is an entrenched institution which is not inclined to change. It is not driven by market forces and does not have a history of research and development integral to its growth and progress.

Therein lies one particular problem: there is no mechanism for growth and progress beyond the individual teacher and the individual decision to change. Much of the reform literature of the last decade has attempted to address this problem (Sizer, Fullan, Sarason), but it remains, nonetheless. And because it does, reform stutters and sputters in many places. Yet there *are* teachers who want to change, who want to venture into new territory, who are willing to take some risks and try some new ideas. This volume is for those people.

There is no doubt in my mind that the *system* needs an overhaul, a radical revision — and there are certainly movements afoot. But what of that classroom practitioner who honestly looks at his or her work and decides things must change? This is the scenario for Ted Sizer's seminal work, *Horace's Compromise*. The dilemma he describes there still applies to many classroom teachers. Is there a point where the individual can decide that the compromises must cease? But, if that decision is made, what then?

What is proposed here is that the individual classroom teacher has always been *the* element in schools which "makes a difference." In that sense, teaching is a unique occupation in our society. You can stop almost any person on the street and ask them to relate a story about a teacher (or teachers) who *had an impact* or made a difference in their life. Of those asked, 95% will, without hesitation, not only tell you the name of some teacher, but also regale you with a story about *how* some teacher's actions had an effect on them. There is no other job in this society with that widespread an influence on the general population. It is an important point, and one that many teachers seldom reflect on. You can't ask for "lawyer" stories, or "accountant" stories, or even "doctor" stories and be relatively **certain** you'll get a response. With teachers — almost always; and almost always *positive*.

Classroom teachers make a difference and, because of it, this volume is aimed at helping individual teachers focus on how they can begin to affect change in their classrooms, whether or not their school or district is undergoing systemic change. The underlying assumption here is that, sooner or later, the school or district *will*, in fact, begin changing. Teachers who have begun the change process will simply be ahead of the game at the very least, or will ultimately be potential leaders and coaches of larger change initiatives. Either way, it cannot hurt for individual teachers to begin reflecting on their classroom practice and considering *how* they might conduct their own research and development to improve the teaching/learning environment for their students. This chapter provides guidelines for those teachers inclined to change, but unsure of where to begin or what direction to head in. It is a map, really, proposing several routes leading to the *territory ahead*.

CLASSROOM SKYDIVING

If one sets out to change one's classroom practice in a school where systemic change is not the order of the day, the analogy to skydiving seems appropriate. The teacher who has decided to consider change has probably thought about attempting something which is seen by others as "risky," and not entirely logical or practical — it is not something one *has to* do. Nonetheless, something has led the individual to decide that this is an experience which should be tried, for whatever reason — some sense of adventure, as a way to inject some thrill into a routine existence, or maybe because it will be a great story to tell others or write about.

Once the decision has been made, and you're up in the plane, there is a point of no return. The parachute is on, the plane is up, you've been coached on what to do, and the moment of truth arrives. The door opens, the wind is whistling by, and, somehow, you leave the plane and enter free fall. Exhilaration, anxiety, and adrenaline fight for attention — the thrill of the freedom and speed mix with the apprehension about whether the parachute will open. A million thoughts and feelings rush by, the sensations are physical and mental and a blur. And then, somehow, the cord is pulled, the 'chute jerks open, and you're floating down, able to relax, somewhat, as you guide yourself to earth.

Individuals who embark on changing their classroom, who decide to move into areas of classroom practice that are new and untried (at least in *their* school), are educational skydivers. They've read literature about change, they've attended workshops and conferences (they've met other skydivers who've lived to tell about it, in essence), they've thought about "doing it" themselves, and, finally, have made a decision to take the plunge. If they are reading this book, they're at the airstrip and about to get some coaching and practice jumps in a safe, protected environment. If they take what is presented here back to their classroom, they've left the runway with their parachute strapped on and are about to experience the thrills and chills of performance assessment free fall — with the same exhilaration and anxiety the skydiver feels.

The difference, of course, is that moving into new classroom assessment practices isn't potentially life-threatening (though some might argue to the contrary), and, while the skydiver is taking a personal risk, there is also a sense that a teacher is pushing his or her students out of the plane, too. The argument I make to counter that dramatic charge is this: If performance assessment is **thoughtfully** implemented, students only stand to gain from the practice. But the idea that the teacher will somehow "bring down" the students with this kind of "experiment" is a powerful obstacle for some, and needs to be addressed.

QUESTIONING ASSUMPTIONS: TURNING ROADBLOCKS INTO SPEED-BUMPS

Everything we do, and particularly those things we engage in which are connected to institutions, operates around sets of assumptions, mental models, and paradigms which dictate *how* we proceed.

Because institutions like the church, the government, and the school, are foundational in our society — and because they have long histories — the assumptions which govern the institutions often go unquestioned. Basic questions like "Why do we do that this way?" and "Who decided this?" go unanswered *because they are never asked!* For those who are considering classroom skydiving, the first exercise in preparation is a simple one: Question the Assumptions.

In a wonderful book (published in 1971 and now out-of-print), *How to Survive in Your Native Land*, James Herndon sums up the assumption-questioning problem most teachers and schools face. In an "Explanatory Note" entitled *No Man*, Herndon describes classic dreams/nightmares teachers have. He then explains why he thinks people have these dreams.

> They occur to people who do not imagine that it is they themselves who determine what happens wherever it is they work. Teachers imagine that they determine nothing. Who built the school? Not the teachers. Who decided that there would be thirty-eight desks in each room? Not the teachers. Who decided that thirty-eight kids in Room 3 ought to learn about Egypt in the seventh grade from 10:05 to 10:50? Not the teachers. Who decided that there ought to be forty-five minutes for lunch and that there ought to be stewed tomatoes in those plastic containers? Not the teachers. Who decided about the curriculum and who decided about the textbooks? Not us. Not us! All we know is that we have this room and thirty-eight desks and thirty-eight kids come in and if there are thirty-eight desks it's perfectly clear that the thirty-eight kids belong in the thirty-eight desks and therefore ought to sit down in them, and if we have thirty-eight books of one sort or another it's obvious that each of the thirty-eight kids ought to get one, and now that they have one it's also logical that we ought to assign something to read and do in them, and in order to do that we have to talk, and if some kids talk while we talk we get to explain the logic of the situation to them at length just as I have done here, and then having assigned something it's apparent that we ought to collect the assignments and. . . .
>
> We feel we have nothing to with it, beyond the process of managing what is presented to us. Presented to us by

whom? The principal? But the principal tells us . . . this is the situation, he didn't invent it, we all must only live with it. The superintendent? He gives us an inspiring speech on opening day, but beyond that makes it clear that our problems are not his invention. . . The board of education? The state board? The superintendent of public instruction? No, man, they didn't do it. Who decided that Egypt is just right for seventh graders? Who decided that DNA must be something which all kids answer questions about? Who decided that California Indians must enter the world of fourth grade kids, or that South America must be "learned" by sixth graders?

Nobody, it seems, made any of these decisions. Noman did it. Noman is responsible for them. The people responsible for the decisions about how schools ought to go are dead. Very few people are able to ask questions of dead men. So we treat those decisions precisely as if dead men made them, as if none of them are up to us live people to make, and therefore we determine that we are not responsible for them. It ain't our fault! It ain't our fault!

Herndon, pp. 100–102

Herndon's implication, then, is that assumptions go unchallenged because we can't figure out who to ask about how they were arrived at. For our purposes, it doesn't matter who decided anything: the Classroom Skydiving candidate, if (s)he is to be successful, has to begin by questioning *all* the basic assumptions that affect his or her classroom. What we will examine here are five assumptions which commonly block teachers from attempting change. An explicit purpose of presenting this challenge to these assumptions is to help people see that what is often described as a *roadblock* can easily be reduced to a *speed bump* if we simply question the assumptions upon which the roadblock is built.

QUESTIONING THE ASSUMPTIONS

We focus on five recurrent assumptions which invariably emerge when teachers are faced with the prospect of changing classroom practice. After stating the assumptions (and certainly there are far more than *five* underlying the nature and structure of schools), it is important to carefully examine what the assumptions are *really* saying about school and *why* they are saying it. In the critical process, some faulty reasoning may be uncovered, as well as some reasons to do *exactly opposite* of what the assumption proposes.

- ◆ *Assumption 1.* We've always done it this way, why change?
- ◆ *Assumption 2.* The public/community wants it this way.
- ◆ *Assumption 3.* I don't have the time (to change).
- ◆ *Assumption 4.* I have to get *them* ready for the {SATs, Regents, MEAPs, etc.}
- ◆ *Assumption 5.* What if it doesn't work? Then what?

ASSUMPTION 1: WE'VE ALWAYS DONE IT THIS WAY. WHY CHANGE?

The problem with this assumption is that it presumes that the way "we've always done it" is working well. There is compelling evidence to the contrary at this point. The American secondary school curriculum was first designed in 1893 and "reevaluated" in the 1920s. There has been little change in the basic structure of that curriculum in the time that has passed.

Let's consider some evidence about why we should question this assumption. America, in 1893 and 1920, was a very different nation than it is today. An emerging industrial giant, faced with floods of immigrants from eastern and southern Europe, the dominant model for organizational development was the factory system. Popularized by Henry Ford's success, the idea that a "product" could be assembled along a conveyor belt by adding the component pieces bit-by-bit became the prevailing metaphor for the age. And secondary schools adopted it, adding several other "real world" concepts to create the basic system we still see today.

The fragmented curriculum, following the college model (the 1893 designers were, for the most part, college presidents), broke knowledge into pieces: History, Literature, Science, and Mathematics as the "major" core, with Foreign Language, Art, Music, and Physical Education as "minor" offerings. The scientific management of factories dictated how time could be used "efficiently," so an easy formula for the school day evolved: seven classes plus lunch taught between 8:00 a.m. and 3:00 p.m. basically breaks into eight 40–48 minutes (with "passing time" built in) sections. Like the raw material moving down the conveyor, students would move from one class to another, having the appropriate "part" added so as to become a finished "product."

An adjunct of the factory model, too, was that students should be sorted and selected; that is, the future "managers" should be distinguished from the future "laborers," so as to be appropriately prepared for the places in society. Thus, homogeneous tracking was born. *How* students were tracked (even to this day) related as much to race, gender, ethnicity, and socioeconomic status as to any "intelligence" students may have exhibited. In fact, much early school tracking was based on the administration of Binet's "IQ" testing — a purpose the French scientist *specifically noted* his test **should not** be used for! Yet this is all part of the "we've always done it this way" assumption.

An interesting note regarding this assumption and the curriculum, too, has to do with the order of courses in high schools. Why is the sequence of mathematics invariably *Algebra, Geometry, Trigonometry,* and science *Biology, Chemistry, Physics*? If you examine the proposal from the 1893 Committee of Ten you discover that various subjects were "recommended" but that local districts were encouraged to decide what sequence courses should be presented in. The Committee, in fact, listed all courses in *every* discipline in **alphabetical order** (History: American, British, Greek, Roman; Literature: American, British, French, German). Yet arguments will be made that the math and science curriculum *has to be* taught in the alphabetical order it was presented in over a century ago. Unchallenged, unquestioned assumptions; rules made by dead people we can't talk to.

A final note: Think about objects and ideas you deal with *every day* in the mid-1990s which didn't exist as commonplace 10–15 years ago. Personal computers, cable television, cellular phones, fax machines, and a host of other technological, as well as ideological (the fall of the U.S.S.R., the shift in South Africa), objects and ideas were not on the scene or the horizon a decade or so ago. A simple question: How old were today's secondary students 10–15 years ago? The oldest were 3 or 4 years old. Many weren't born or are too young to even know a world in which this technology and political alignment didn't existed. Nonetheless, they attend a school designed a century ago.

ASSUMPTION 2: THE PUBLIC WANTS IT.

Schools try to be responsive to their constituencies. This is one reason we see "new" curriculum packages and "new" textbooks flooding classrooms on a regular basis. There is a belief that schools have to "keep up with" these "new" ideas and that the public wants the best for its children. There is no doubt that the sentiment connected to these actions is accurate. But, too often, the actions are performed as a reflex to some pressure, to one small interest group which is particularly vocal, or a "change" is wrought because a new superintendent wants to leave his or her mark on the district. Classroom teachers are well aware of all this. Nonetheless, an assumption which often goes unquestioned, particularly regarding curriculum, instruction, and assessment, is that "the public wants it" the way it is. The question which needs to be asked, and then pursued, is, "When was the last time we checked, and who did we check with?"

How aware is "the public" of the shifting conceptions of intelligence which have gained acceptance and notoriety (in the worlds of psychology and education) in the last 10 years? How current are most members of "the public" regarding debates about tracking and assessment? How often is "the public" invited into the school to actually see what is going on in classrooms? The answer to these questions is well-known to anyone who has worked in schools: the public is little aware, has no clear notion of the arguments in educational debates, and seldom, if ever, is in school *for a full day* to see what actually goes on.

These are significant points. If schools are to be responsive to the public, then the public must be educated as to what is really going on, not only in their schools, but in the world of education. If schoolpeople (teachers, administrators, etc.) do not develop an open dialogue with the public, if traditional, adversarial, roles are maintained, little can be examined to bring about thoughtful and effective change in schools.

Very often, "the public wants it" the way it is because they have a rather inaccurate and nostalgic memory of what school was, or they adopt an attitude that "it was good enough for me, it's good enough for you." Neither of these particularly helps our students improve their performance or escape from what it often a stultifying and depressing experience.

The public wants quality education — that is a cry which is heard loud and clear. Yet, who is defining the terms here? "Quality" in terms of what? The colleges we send our students to? The proven literacy of our graduates? The ability to use computers by *all* students? Without genuine dialogue and thoughtful exchange about what the purpose of our local school is, about what essential outcomes students need to know and be able to do, without careful study of "what works" and "what doesn't," it is difficult to believe anyone **really** knows what "the public wants."

The argument here is twofold: (1) Reality check — what does the public *really* want? (2) What will it take to develop a school culture in which genuine, honest **dialogue** can be created between all the significant constituencies the school is supposed to serve? These are awesome tasks and, quite possibly, daunting. It is easier to *assume* we know what "the public wants" than to actually find out the facts and develop a dialogue. Yet, without that, all we know is that schools will continue to plod along just as they are, fulfilling the desires of an amorphous "public" which has not been included in the dialogue about the schools charged with educating their children.

ASSUMPTION 3: I DON'T HAVE THE TIME

Time is always the great enemy in school — there's never enough time to do "what we have to do." Yet this is another unquestioned assumption. How *is* time used — and what for? Are we being rationale, thoughtful, productive, and efficient with time in schools? Much depends on your perspective regarding what needs to be done, as well as *how* it needs to be done. Let's consider the basic organization of the school day.

We have already looked at how the day was divided according to the factory/industrial model. Seven classes plus lunch divided between 7 hours creates the basic eight-period day, 45-minute period model. But let's consider this structure in light of how the rest of the world operates. What business would ask its employees to get up every 45 minutes, stop what they're working on, and move to a new task with a new supervisor? Worse, what if the supervisors seldom, if ever, talked to each other about what they had the employees working on? Of course it sounds ludicrous to consider asking adults in a "real world" business situation to operate in this fashion.

Employees would complain and the companies would quickly go out of business. But the tyranny of having to "cover" **all** the material between September and June requires that teachers and students operate in a situation which is designed for confusion and inefficiency. Nonetheless, the rigid six-, seven-, eight-, and sometimes nine-period day schedules dominate schools just as they did in the early years of this century. Given that scenario, is it any wonder that teachers believe they don't have the time to consider new methods or techniques, much less a radical overhaul of the system?

So, what can the individual classroom teacher do, given this situation? First, he or she must step back and consider the situation realistically, element by element. A systematic analysis of outcome-goals (what's *essential* for students to know and be able to do by June?), a realistic evaluation of course content (in terms of what students can actually *learn* given their developmental level, prior knowledge, etc.), and a careful examination of the assessments which are used to provide clear feedback regarding student learning are the keys to "stealing Time" and creating a more engaging and productive learning environment.

WHAT'S ESSENTIAL FOR STUDENTS TO KNOW AND BE ABLE TO DO?

While this is becoming a hackneyed piece of jargon (politicians on C-Span are using it!), it remains *the* essential question for teachers to ask. It goes right to the heart of schooling: what's our purpose? What are students supposed to *leave* school with? Presently, diplomas are simply certificates of attendance, for the most part. Without clarity about outcomes, without plans to design curriculum, and assessments which will provide *evidence* and *artifacts* of student progress toward or attainment of those outcomes, time will inevitably be an overwhelming obstacle. If a teacher's main focus is on content, and the *amount* of that content is what drives the curriculum, then time is an almost impossible barrier. But, if teachers can relieve themselves of the notion that they *have to "cover" everything* between September and June, if they can honestly look at what's worth knowing as regards their domain, they may find there is much more time to teach. By leaving the mile-wide/inch-deep traditional curriculum and adopting a system which asks students to demonstrate they have learned essential skills and content knowledge *with depth*, teachers can begin designing curriculum, instruction, and assessment which, ultimately, is more time efficient. This can be difficult, however, because it bumps up against Assumption 4.

ASSUMPTION 4: I HAVE TO GET THEM READY FOR THE TEST!

Whether it's the SAT's, the New York State Regents, the Departmental midterm, or some other standardized, "objective" examination, the testing-dog tail wags the school and controls the lives of many teachers. The most telling question I can think of is one Grant Wiggins is fond of asking: "If students take the test *one year later* — without your course 'in front of' it — how will they do?" Most teachers will honestly answer, "Not very well." The next, more important, question is, "What did the students learn, then?"

If our objective is to teach people to "cram," to spend 150 or 160 days preparing to sit for 3 hours to "achieve" on some test in a subject they retain little or nothing about, how can we claim students are learning in our schools? Without asking students to genuinely exhibit what they know in meaningful ways, creating artifacts and evidence of their learning, then we can't make any claims about what schools are accomplishing. But how can the individual classroom teacher fight the monolith that is testing in this country?

One suggestion would be to look at tests students are asked to take and do a careful item analysis of the questions. There are, undoubtedly, a number of items which coincide with outcomes the teacher would be aiming for. It should be no problem to prepare students for those items. But what of the others? Do we *have to* spend the bulk of our days preparing students for questions which do not relate to outcomes we believe are important? The answer is a simple "Yes" and "No."

Let me illustrate by way of example. The Advanced Placement American History test asks 100 multiple-choice questions, a "free-response" essay (which provides five choices), and a document-based question. If an outcome for an American History course is that students actually learn to work like historians, the document-based question provides a fair and challenging format to design authentic work around. If we want students to be able to respond articulately in writing to a general question about trends or events in American History, the free-response essay provides an adequate format for that. But what about the 100 multiple choice questions? Here's a strategy.

If we accept that the test is a fair one and that the 100 questions will not be trivial, we can ask students to first consider that premise. It's a fair test which wants to see some knowledge of specific content between the years 1607 and 1990. Using textbooks and other general American History reference resources, ask students to work in small groups and determine what people, events, or important ideas *would have to be* on a **fair** test in American History. Each group should compile a list of at least 75 names, events, etc. Students should then post their lists and do some simple compare/contrast work to develop a final class-list of 100 items they believe would *have to be asked* on a fair test of American History knowledge. From there it's easy. Designate one day each week as "10-question quiz day" and drill-and-kill those 100 items until May, spending 4 out of 5 days doing authentic historiography, debates, simulations, and so on.

If you ride the subways in New York City you can't help but notice signs for a company which promises "Higher scores or your money back." Meeting two to three times a week for 6 weeks, this company makes a handsome profit each year preparing students in *test-taking strategies and skills.* My contention is that professional teachers should be able to do exactly the same thing. Decide to prepare students for whatever test looms over your head by using the least amount of time with them as is necessary developing their *test-taking* skills, while spending most of your time doing authentic, in-depth work in whatever discipline you teach. The students will "achieve" on the test and will learn far more during the non-"Quiz Day" time.

ASSUMPTION 5: WHAT IF IT DOESN'T WORK?

The underlying "given" in this assumption is an interesting one: *Everything* I do now works very well, *all 180 days* of the school year — how can I "risk" something not working? The implicit statement is that we are doing the best we can do in the best of all possible worlds. Anyone who has worked in a classroom knows how ludicrous this idea is. More significantly, most districts have a mission statement or "philosophy" which asserts that students will be "lifelong learners" and "risk takers." The *what if it doesn't work* assumption paints teachers into a corner — **they** will neither take risks nor model lifelong learning behavior.

Once again, stepping back and looking at what goes on in our classrooms day-in and day-out may help teachers reconsider this assumption. How many lessons *don't* work? And of those that do, are they reaching *the majority* of the students we are teaching? Are students genuinely *engaged* by the work they are currently doing? Do they find relevance, connections, and meaning in the tasks they are asked to fulfill? Or is school a humdrum march *covering* material which will be forgotten over a summer? These are important questions which directly confront Assumption 5.

If, in fact, we are *not* successful every day, if we are not able to genuinely and accurately gauge how much *real* learning is occurring in our classrooms, why can't we take a risk and try alternative approaches (which may become our mainstream approaches, over time)? *Individual* teachers can make that decision. While the fragmentation of the curriculum and the separation of teachers from one another impedes professional development, it *does* provide for a significant amount of autonomy for the individual. While people often invoke the cry, "The STATE says we have to . . . ," I have never, in 23 years of classroom teaching, seen a "State" official in a school inspecting classrooms to make sure some curriculum or assessment is being "properly" implemented. In fact, there are no Curriculum Police out there. It is another reality check which is never made, except by those who are willing to take the risk of challenging assumptions — those willing to skydive in their classroom.

HOW TO SHIFT PRACTICE:
FROM CONTENT COVERAGE TO ESSENTIAL QUESTIONS

The importance of clearly focusing on what students need to know and be able to do has already been mentioned. If we are not clear about those outcomes, nothing else can really ensue regarding teaching and learning. We will simply move through a textbook or a curriculum guide, *covering* lower-order thinking skills in content-knowledge, comprehension, and application. If we want our students to move into the higher-order thinking skills of analysis, synthesis, and evaluation, however, we need to consider looking at curriculum, instruction, and assessment from a new perspective.

The old paradigm of "curriculum → instruction → testing" is a linear one in which content-knowledge, primarily, is transmitted to students by the teacher. This has been called the mug-jug approach (students are empty vessels to be filled with knowledge by teachers) and the "banking theory" (*see* Paolo Friere, *The Pedagogy of the Oppressed*) in which teachers make "deposits" into empty accounts (students), slowly building up the capital "saved." In a world in which accumulated information is doubling every 2½ years, this is clearly a losing proposition. One look at ever-expanding Biology textbooks vividly makes the point: Could any 10th-grader ever *really learn* all that material? More poignantly: Do we know any adults who know all that? Because knowledge is expanding and multi-faceted, the myth that there is a finite body of knowledge which can be "mastered" needs to be dispelled. If we do that, however, what replaces it?

Theodore Sizer, the chairman of the Coalition of Essential Schools, proposed a different approach to curriculum in *Horace's Compromise* (1984) and *Horace's School* (1992). Sizer is clearly a direct descendent of John Dewey and other progressive educators from the early part of the century — his is a student-centered, student-active approach. At the heart of the curriculum-instruction-assessment trinity, in the Coalition's approach, is the "essential question."

Proposed by Sizer and refined by then Director of Research Grant Wiggins, the essential question approach looks at curriculum-instruction-assessment as a fluid circle of components, not easily separated from one another. Their common link are questions which drive student (and teacher) inquiry. Their goal is to develop "habits of mind" in students — traits which will long outlive a summer away from classrooms.

Following the outcome-based, planning backwards model, this approach focuses on several key "habits" which students work on throughout their academic career.

- **Evidence**: How do we know what we know? What's the evidence and how credible is it?

+ **Viewpoint**: From whose perspective are we seeing/hearing/reading? From what angle or perspective? Whose voice are we hearing? From where is the statement or image coming?

+ **Connections**: How are things, events, or people connected to each other? What is the cause and what is the effect? How do things fit together? What else do we know that fits with this?

+ **Conjecture**: What's new and what's old? Have we run across this before? What if . . . ? Could it have been otherwise? Are there alternatives?

+ **Relevance**: So what? Why does it matter? What does it all mean? What difference does it make? Who cares? Why should *I* care?

This basic set of questions serves as an umbrella under which more focused essential questions are developed by teachers — questions which drive specific curriculum in specific directions. So, while students will always be looking for "answers" to the habits of mind essential questions, their immediate coursework will be driven by more specific questions.

For example, an American History course might focus on questions like: What *is* the American Dream? Does a nation "come of age" the way people do? What are the characteristics or nature of revolution? What makes something uniquely American? A Biology course might ask: How do physical systems in humans compare to systems that run a city? What is essential to plant and animal life? How are patterns in nature and patterns in humans similar or different? In English, we might ask: What makes a good story? What determines the actions of people? What makes a story artistic? Who determines what good writing is? In mathematics, these questions might drive a course: How many ways can a problem be solved? What is precision (in measurement, in time, in calculations) — and how do we know? Is music a mathematic or artistic system? In Physical Education, students might be challenged with these questions: Are there physical limits to human achievement? How can scientific knowledge improve athletic accomplishment? How are games invented?

One tenet of the Coalition of Essential Schools is that "less is more," regarding content coverage and approaching teaching/learning. By focusing students on *questions* aimed at outcomes of significance, teachers can choose content which best suits the instruction and assessment of student progress toward the goal. In that way, curriculum, instruction, and assessment become inextricably linked, connected by the driving questions. The result is an *active* classroom, characterized by inquiry, a place where the Coalition's aphorism "student-as-worker, teacher-as-coach" becomes reality.

But how are essential questions developed? Some basic guidelines are helpful. As articulated by Grant Wiggins, the criteria for essential questions are:

◆ They point to the heart of a subject or topic, especially its controversies.

◆ They generate multiple plausible answers, perspectives, and research directions — leading to other questions.

◆ They cast old knowledge, ideas, texts in a new light; they make the familiar strange or the strange familiar.

◆ They lead to discovery and *uncoverage*, as opposed to "coverage."

◆ They engender further and deepening interest in the subject.

◆ They are provocative, enticing, and engagingly framed.

Wiggins also suggests that essential questions should be designed to highlight oddities, historical controversies, counterintuitive facts, and dilemmas. Those guidelines provide an entry point for teacher-thinking about what content would be best to use: is it counterintuitive? A genuine dilemma? An oddity? Wiggins also points out that essential questions can be derived from themes or topics teachers may already employ.

The word of caution here would be: If one chooses to transform a current topic/theme unit into an essential question unit, expect to **cut** some other topic/theme from the curriculum altogether — less *is* more. An essential question unit will take more time, delve deeper, and drive student inquiry in unpredictable, but valuable, directions. As a result, there will be less time to "cover" everything you may have in the past. This **is not** a simple substitution program being proposed here — this is a *complete break into new territory*. This is a paradigm shift, a new direction.

Initially, the individual teacher who wishes to explore designing an essential question unit might want to focus on a topic or text which the teacher sees as particularly rich. The teacher should *immediately* evaluate what other topic or text can be dropped from the curriculum. If you are shifting to this approach, you **will not be able** to "cover" everything you cover now. Honestly and realistically consider what should stay and what can go. What's *essential* to your course? What will best move students toward outcomes they need to exhibit?

Once you have wrestled with those hard decisions, Wiggins recommends that you consider your topics and texts in the following light:

> If course content can be thought of as "answers" to key questions, what are the questions? What questions have been central to arguments and debates over time on this topic? (*Workshop* handout, 1994)

Again, this is a "backwards-planning" approach: When have we thought to consider course content as answers to questions as our *first step* in planning instruction and assessment? Yet this opens the door to developing questions which will drive student inquiry. If we consider the content a mere jumping-off point for developing *questions* which will guide our curriculum, if we consider what questions the authors were trying to solve (Wiggins, *Workshop*, 1994), we can begin to look at curriculum, instruction, and assessment in an entirely new light.

This is not easily done and it means teachers have to move into territory which has often gone unexplored. The work is "messy" because it is not as simple as presenting a body of content-knowledge and hoping the students "get it." The focus of work in the classroom shifts from the teacher to the students, to a far more constructivist approach in which students are asked to make sense and meaning of problems, to probe questions and raise their own. It is a risk, moving away from a familiar landscape of content delivery into the unknown wilderness of student engagement and inquiry. But, as with any other pioneering endeavor, the rewards can be great, the new land fertile, and the satisfaction deep.

WHERE TO BEGIN

So where can the individual classroom teacher begin if the teacher is interested in moving into the realm of performance assessments? What needs to be considered? What resources are available? What are the easiest avenues to make the initial forays down?

First, one has to examine one's present practice. What's most nettlesome? What unquestioned assumptions need to be challenged? What is it you really want to *make sure* your students have genuinely learned? How will you acquire evidence of their learning which is compelling?

At the end of this chapter is a template for planning backwards. It provides general guidelines for focusing teachers' work. The first rough spot will be shedding the impulse to *cover* material. A recent study of schools using performance assessments showed that students *were* doing more authentic work more often, but teachers were still caught in the bind of *covering content* — essentially increasing their workload. Consider this: What **content** knowledge did you retain from your high school courses? People who were "A" students in Chemistry can't even recall that they had to balance equations in that class (a conversation overheard in a faculty room). So, first and foremost, reconsider what's *essential* regarding the selection and amount of content that needs to be "covered." Force yourself to think about what your course would be like *without* certain content units. If this hurdle cannot be overcome, it will be very difficult to successfully implement performance assessments and not burn out.

Next, avail yourself of resources that are already out there. The last chapter in this book presents critiques of a number of books and publications which can help guide the classroom practitioner into this new territory. This approach challenges another assumption which is woven into the fabric of schools: teachers are "experts" and, if not, can "adapt" to new methods or materials very quickly.

This backhanded compliment flies in the face of what we know about professional knowledge and lifelong learning. Who would seek the services of a surgeon who was noted for "learning" some new technique over a weekend — or even over a summer? The need for *reflective practice* as a norm, and not an exception, is fundamental to moving into performance assessments. As such, one seeks out as much material about new methods and techniques as possible, reads carefully, discusses new thoughts and ideas with others, and then carefully plans any new practice.

Planning should *build-in* the greatest possibilities for success. Teachers have been asked and expected, for too long, to "adopt and adapt" any new idea that has come down the pike. It is time to turn that style around by developing the thoughtful habits of reflective practice.

The following chapters present two methods of assessment which any classroom teacher can implement. They do not require school-wide change or site-based committees to consider them. In fact, these have been done in K–12 classrooms for a number of years now. There may be someone *in your school* employing these methods already! Starting a dialogue about what you are considering may "expose" other risk-takers who have begun to head down the path to performance assessments.

Portfolio assessment and Socratic seminars have been used successfully in classrooms for so long, it is difficult to term them "innovations." They are methods which can be used by teachers in any discipline area and are, by design, learner-centered. They can be adapted to the most traditional settings and allow classroom practitioners the opportunity to develop assessments which produce compelling evidence of authentic student learning. They are **not** magic bullets or panaceas. Teachers must investigate carefully *how* they want to implement these assessments because there will be a direct impact on curriculum and instruction. But the opportunity is there.

Implementation of new assessments is difficult in any setting, but it is not impossible. Thoughtful planning, careful preparation, and clear commitment are essential ingredients. Initially, the risks seem great — like the skydiving scenario described earlier. But the potential rewards, in terms of student achievement and learning, are far greater. This book offers guidelines and examples for those teachers who are ready to take the leap. What you will discover is a sky full of colleagues who have made the same decision. So, cinch up, take a deep breath, and prepare for takeoff.

3

PORTFOLIO ASSESSMENT: THE "MULTIPLE CHOICE" OF PERFORMANCE ASSESSMENT

The best known and most commonly used performance assessment is the portfolio. Those teachers and schools which have been using the writing process have used portfolio approaches for a number of years. Even though widely used, if you asked five different teachers to define portfolio assessment, you could easily receive five different answers — none of which would be "wrong." Such is the nature of portfolio assessment. There are many possibilities and they are often tailored to the specific situation or school one finds them in. No matter how they may be compiled, there are several basic approaches to creating portfolios.

The best known portfolio system is the one which artists and photographers use, the best-works portfolio. In this system, the person submitting the portfolio assembles his or her best work in a certain area. The photographer, for example, submits the best portrait, the best landscape, the best color photograph, the best black-and-white shot, the best journalistic photograph, the best sports-action picture, and so on. A best-works portfolio is designed to show off the exemplary work of the person submitting it and the choices, as to what is submitted, are made by the person presenting the portfolio.

A *selection* portfolio is one in which the submissions are decided by both the person whose work will be on display and the person or persons to whom the portfolio is submitted. Using the same photographer's work, we might find examples of some (or all) of the best works material, but would also find more, or other examples, of work, as requested by those receiving the portfolio. So, a newspaper publisher might want to see several examples of journalistic and sports photography, caring little for the portrait or landscape work. In a school setting, a teacher may request certain, specific assignments be included in the portfolio — and may even select those pieces him- or herself.

The *process* portfolio is one which contains a span of work from an early stage to a finished product. Again, our photographer may be asked to submit contact sheets, proofs, a variety of developed pictures which illustrate the photographer's talents in using darkroom methods to create different effects, and a series of final photographs. Those teachers engaged in writing process work use a similar method, asking students to submit brainstorming notes, first outlines, early drafts, edited and reedited drafts, and a final composition.

Teachers developing portfolios with their students may well use some hybrid from these three areas, and certainly there's no hard and fast rule as to which should or must be used. What is crucial, however, is being clear as to what the purpose of the portfolio is, who **the audience** for the portfolio is, **how** the portfolio will be used, and what **the benefits** to the student will be. To simply "collect" student work and put it in a folder is not portfolio assessment. A random — or even "planned" — collection of graded work, loosely connected in a manila folder does not a portfolio system make. Let's consider what might go into a student's portfolio and why those items would be selected.

WHAT'S THE PURPOSE?

Before designing a portfolio system for classroom, grade-level, schoolwide, or districtwide use, serious consideration must be given to why such a system should be implemented. What purpose or purposes will the portfolio system serve? Because there is a certain familiarity with the concept, as evidenced by the artist/photography example, it is all too easy to simply say, "Let's use portfolios." Such snap decisions can easily contribute to creating yet another requirement for students with no clear purpose in mind. In fact, a problem with performance assessments in general is that they often become "add-on's" to the curriculum, instruction, and testing which already exists in schools. This, once again, opens the can of worms which new forms of assessment cannot avoid: *Changing assessment practice requires a total rethinking of how we organize curriculum, instruction, scheduling , and a host of other institutional issues.* And so it is with portfolio assessment. Because the concept is accessible to State Departments of Education, Superintendents, Building Principals, Department Chairs, and the like, it is possible that portfolios can be mandated from above — to illustrate to the public that a State or District is moving in "new directions" with assessment. Needless to say, this is not the way a portfolio system should be developed. However, even if one were faced with a top-down mandate to institute such a system, there is no reason why a *thoughtful* and *thought-provoking* portfolio system could not be designed. Let's consider what that would mean.

First and foremost, as with any performance assessment, what do we want our students to know and be able to do — and how might a portfolio system serve those ends? Secondly, how will a portfolio be used by teachers and students, once assembled? Portfolios can serve as valuable assessment tools for both students and teachers — but their purpose must be clear *before* their implementation. Clarity of purpose will help shape the final design of the portfolio system a teacher or district will employ. Given the possibilities for that design, then, what is it we want to know about students and what is it we want our students to learn about themselves?

A primary value in working with portfolio assessments is that they allow students to learn to judge their own progress. This assumes an important factor is in place, however: students clearly know what is expected of them. Again, an issue of changed practice is raised — student achievement is gauged along a continuum of progress rather than by periodic auditing of content coverage. Particularly when considering the use of a selection portfolio or a process portfolio, the student becomes the ultimate arbiter of the quality and value of the work submitted. The possibilities for student reflection and self-assessment are of paramount importance when considering the development of a portfolio system. While this is an important issue in the use of portfolios, it leaves an equally important issue for teachers on the table: how can portfolios be used as an evaluative instrument for student work?

Should portfolios be used as an evaluative instrument reflecting student achievement? There is no black-and-white answer to this question. What can be said, though, is that those employing such a system must be clear as to the purpose of the portfolio. If portfolios are to be used to determine grades for students, an important factor is that students, teachers, and parents know how portfolio assessment is used to determine those grades. This requires thoughtful discussions about:

♦   What is included in a portfolio.
♦   What the standards are for the work submitted.
♦   What the criteria are by which work will be judged.
♦   How will those standards and criteria be determined?

This brings the purpose question to the forefront and again raises the issue of changed practice, which, in turn, introduces the concept of known and published standards and criteria which translate into clear expectations and goals for students. Certainly there are examples of this concept in practice, as illustrated later in this chapter, but even those must be seen as works in progress. Because performance assessments, in general, are still in their formative stages, the development of standards, criteria, and scoring rubrics by teachers are in their infancy.

The problem this raises is that the development of new systems occurs in a culture which has never asked teachers or districts to account for their standards. Because norm-referenced, standardized tests have been the yardsticks for judging student and school district performance, it is difficult to convince people, teachers and the public alike, that there may be another way to gauge student achievement. Part of the conversation which must take place, however, must focus on the purpose of assessment itself — be it a standardized test or a portfolio system. Because portfolios are tangible evidence of student work which is judged against known standards, because students can view their own work in light of those standards, the purpose of portfolios becomes evident — continued student improvement toward high standards. So, the community debate over standards and how those standards are created and judged must be an integral part of the development of a portfolio system.

For practical purposes, this discussion can happen at the classroom level between teachers and students, at the faculty level, at a districtwide level, and even on a statewide level. The crucial questions in this discussion return to the issue of purpose: If a portfolio system is developed, what is it designed to accomplish? The important questions shaping such a discussion are:

- What is quality student work?
- What are the essential skills, content, and attitudes students should know and be able to do — and to what level?
- How will student work be evaluated?

While these questions focus on the issue of purpose, the other aspect of portfolio assessment which concerns teachers and students is one of logistics.

WHAT DOES IT LOOK LIKE?

No matter what kind of portfolio system might be developed, some common questions arise:

- What goes into the portfolio — and who decides?
- Who "keeps" the portfolio — teacher, student, a central repository?
- Will the portfolio "follow" the student from grade to grade?

◆   How can we use portfolios to give students grades?

These are all good questions which have no single or simple answer. Unlike standardized assessments, portfolio and other performance assessments are used according to the dictates of the community which implement them.

WHAT GOES INTO THE PORTFOLIO?

What do we want to know about our students? What kinds of work would best reflect their progress toward the achievement of valued goals? What evidence would clearly indicate student growth toward the mastery of essential skills, content, and attitudes? The answers to these questions help determine the design of a portfolio system, whether it's for an individual classroom, a grade-level, a department, or an entire school system. Like portfolios themselves, the design of a portfolio system allows for choices and, like a portfolio system, the design demands purposeful decisions.

As important is the question, "who decides?" The possibility for including students in the portfolio design — especially at the classroom level — is a significant one. A problem with our present evaluation system is one of mystification for students. Imagine if students were included from the start in helping design their assessment instrument. As far as the contents of the portfolio are concerned, consider the possibilities based on the type of portfolio which seems appropriate.

If a best-works portfolio is being designed, what variety of best works should be included? Even if we are considering a subject-specific portfolio, imagine the possibilities.

◆   **Language Arts:** The best pieces of a variety of writing styles — expository, creative (poetry, drama, short story), journalistic (reporting, editorial columnist, reviewer), advertising copy, satire/humor — to name a few.

◆   **Science:** The best laboratory work the student has done; the best original hypothesis developed; the best solution to a scientific problem posed by the instructor; the best position paper on a scientific issue (in the style of those which would be presented to a conference of scientists); the best review of an article from a science magazine or journal; the best log or journal entry from a long-term experiment the student conducted.

♦ **Social Studies:** The best historical research paper written; an account of the best debate or discussion the student was involved in; the best original historical theory posed by the student; the best opinion essay on a historical issue; the best commentary on a current event; the best review of a historical biography the student read.

♦ **Mathematics:** The best solution to a problem posed by the instructor; the best original mathematic theory the student has developed; the best review of a mathematics journal or mathematician's biography the student has written; the best written description of problemsolving (describing the process of solving the problem); a photo, diagram, or concept map of a mathematical idea investigated by the student.

The assumption with any of the foregoing, of course, is that students are involved in a wide variety of activities, maximizing their opportunities for selecting "the best" from any of the categories listed. And those lists are not exhaustive. Best-works portfolios could certainly include "best pieces" of homework, best tests or quizzes, videos of the best group projects students are involved in, and so on. The point, of course, is that students exercise critical judgment in selecting what they believe is their best work. Such a project demands reflective writing (or audiotaping, or videotaping) from the student, explaining the student's selections, and providing the teacher and parents with insight into *how* the student thinks about the subject area the student is submitting the portfolio in.

If we set out to create a selection portfolio, what might we look for? Again, an important decision is who decides what will be selected? And, again, imagine if students were included in this process.

A selection portfolio asks to see a broader span of student work than a best-works portfolio might. Asking students to submit examples of work where they had the most difficulty could be a revealing inclusion. Submissions of several of the same type or style of writing or problemsolving assignments can also be found in selection portfolios. In these instances, we would have created categories which the faculty might design, but allow for student choice in determining what pieces of work are actually included in the portfolio.

With any of these submissions, some form of student reflection would be the value-added component that portfolio assessments bring and which are often missing from more conventional assessments. A selection portfolio collected over a year's time, with items chosen by the student and some, possibly, selected by the teacher can become a deeply reflective compendium of student growth and a highly revealing collection of evidence of genuine achievement.

Selection portfolios, because of their nature, also create opportunities for students and teachers to conference about the work which is going on. Imagine a teacher and student going through the student's work folder together, looking for pieces which fulfill a certain category required in the selection portfolio. The teacher might, quite naturally, "interview" the student during the process, asking why certain pieces of work are chosen rather than others. The teacher might also suggest why the student should consider submitting this or that piece of work, initiating a conversation which brings some new insight to the student about a piece of work. Depending on the outcomes, the selection portfolio becomes a wonderful vehicle for reflection, for developing insight, for creating an evidentiary history of student work, and a host of other significant goals.

In much the same way, a process portfolio can serve significant ends. Because it asks for evidence of developmental work, the process portfolio demands that students examine the step-by-step progress of certain areas of their work. Again, while teachers may define the categories for submission, it remains for the student to become responsible for compiling the necessary work. Most significantly, students become active assessors of their own work and progress. So, in any subject area, teachers can examine which outcomes might best be "measured" by examining student growth and design a process portfolio piece around that. While the most common example of this is in Language Arts, with writing, consider other possible process assessments:

- ◆ Clear documentation of solving a series of laboratory problems in any of the sciences. Students would have to keep running records or logs of their scientific method processes.

- ◆ Double-column mathematics problem solving — where students do their computation/calculation/"figuring" on the left side of the page and later write a running commentary explaining their thought process. (Imagine a series of these focused on a certain kind of problem or problemsolving strategy.)

- ◆ The evolution of a speech or public debate in social studies — from early notes through outlines, research notes, and final draft.

- ◆ the "history" of any piece of artwork, from its original conception (with journals and/or sketches) through first, second, third attempts, and final product.

With any process portfolio, the student's reflective examination of his or her work when the process is completed is clearly the most valuable aspect of this assessment.

HOW DO WE DESIGN ONE?

Depending on what ends are sought, individual classrooms, districts, or even states, will probably use some combination of the types of portfolios described above. Again, the *ends* are what determine our design. By being clear about *what* it is we want to know about our students, and about what we want students to learn about themselves, the Portfolio design begins to take shape. The remainder of this chapter examines four different portfolio assessments: two from classrooms and two used as graduation exhibitions and one from a statewide system which has practical classroom applications. Two are from independent schools and all four are from schools affiliated with the Coalition of Essential Schools — an organization which has been in the forefront of the school reform movement in promoting performance assessments. Through this sampling we can examine how outcomes determine design and how that design can better inform the work of both students and teachers.

CLASSROOM PORTFOLIOS

The most basic unit of schooling is, of course, the classroom. It was mentioned earlier that any classroom teacher can embark on using portfolios, so long as that teacher is thoughtful about purpose and the portfolio design is thought-provoking. Starting at the classroom level, then, we can examine how the individual practitioner can put portfolio assessment to use.

A MATHEMATICS PORTFOLIO

Heathwood Hall Episcopal School is an independent school in Columbia, South Carolina, and a member of the Coalition of Essential Schools. Members of the mathematics department responsible for teaching Algebra I & II and Geometry designed a portfolio project for their students for the 1994–95 school year. The philosophical foundation for their portfolio clearly rests on the new standards issued by the National Council of Teacher of Mathematics (NCTM). These standards are designed to move students away from rote memorization of facts and procedures (focusing on the teacher and textbook as the only sources of knowledge) toward a more student-active, constructivist approach to problemsolving and questioning. Significantly, the NCTM standards and the Heathwood Hall portfolio consider it important that students be able to express their mathematical ideas in writing and orally

Before analyzing the Heathwood Hall math portfolio, let's look at it from the student's point of view; that is, let's examine the project exactly as it is presented to students (Fig. 3.1).

(Text continues on page 42.)

FIGURE 3.1: MATH PORTFOLIO, HEATHWOOD HALL

YOUR MATH PORTFOLIO

D. Venables
A. Haviland
A. Venables
C. Haigler

ALGEBRA I
GEOMETRY
ALGEBRA II
1994-1995

INTRODUCTION

As you know, this year you will be required to maintain a mathematics portfolio. The purpose of this is many-fold: (i) to keep track of your progress in learning math, (ii) to allow you the opportunity to show us what you know and what you've learned in math in ways different from usual tests and quizzes and homework assignments, and (iii) to help you develop skills not typically learned in traditional math classes such as reading and writing within the subject of mathematics. Also, math portfolios allow you to delve into interesting math topics that are not in our class textbook, and they allow you to explore these topics at a depth that is tailored to your ability and interest.

POINTS OF FOCUS

Your math portfolio will focus on the following points:

Problem Solving (developing and executing strategies)
Connections (relating mathematics to other subjects)
Mathematical Communication (reading and writing in mathematics)
Technology (using computers and graphing calculators)
Teamwork (working cooperatively with others toward a common goal)
Growth Over Time (learning from your mistakes)
Mathematical Disposition (developing healthy attitudes about the subject)

OVERVIEW

Each of the first three* quarters your portfolio will contain **five** entries. **Two** of these, Entries #4 and #5 will not vary; the other **three** will vary from one quarter to the next. We call these entry types "Floating" Entries. You will have five types of "Floating" Entries to choose from; all five types are to be completed by the end of the third quarter. The entry types are detailed below.

Individual entries will be assigned <u>due dates throughout the quarter</u>, and your teacher may collect and grade entries anytime after the specified due dates.

Approximately every other double period (or the equivalent thereof), you will be given classtime to work on your portfolios. Your teacher will act as a coach as you work.

---

*For the fourth quarter, you and your classmates will complete a mini-exhibition in lieu of doing portfolio work. Your teacher will discuss this requirement more fully later in the year.

It is important to remember that your portfolio grade is 20% of your quarter grade. Portfolios turned in late will be reduced by 1.5 grade points (maximum grade of 2.5). Remember, too, that producing quality portfolio work is a requirement for this course and that credit for the course, in part, depends on your portfolio.

ENTRY TYPES
"Floating" Entries #1 & #2 & #3 (All categories to be completed by 3rd quarter)

Non-Routine Problem/Puzzle
These problems/puzzles require you to combine or invent problem solving strategies that are different than textbook procedures in order to solve them. They may or may not be related to topics studied in class. A detailed solution, complete with source(s), will be submitted.

Application Entry
This entry will demonstrate an authentic use of mathematics in another subject area including the Fine Arts. Math concepts, principles, and procedures will be employed in a well-grounded, real-world context. Some aspect of this entry will explain the math content, the content from the other subject, and the connection between the two.

Mathematics in Historical Context Entry
This entry requires researching and summarizing in your own words one of the following: (i) a biography of a famous mathematician, (ii) the mathematics of a particular (Non-Western) culture, or (iii) the evolution of mathematical ideas in some branch of mathematics. Sources must be cited.

Math Lab Entry
This entry is an inductive search for an answer to a question *of yours*. It is a guided exploration that leads to a generalization, a concept, or a mathematical relationship between variables.   This will require conjecturing, gathering data, examining models, viewing examples and counter-examples, and drawing conclusions based on your evidence. A report of your process and your findings is required. In each course, all students will work on their math labs during a week set aside for this entry. More information will follow.

Reading & Writing Entry   (quarterly for Algebra II, one quarter for others)
You will read a math-related essay (see your teacher if you are unsure what is covered by this). Then, you will write in your own words what you read complete with either (i) examples from the reading and at least one example of your own, or (ii) some original connection of this topic to some other topic. Consider your audience to be someone in our class; write as if you are explaining this topic to a friend. Sources must be cited.

"Fixed" Entry #4

Progress Entry

With each Portfolio submission, all tests and quizzes taken to date will be submitted in chronology _with corrections_. Test/quiz corrections will be completed on separate paper and include a detailed, revised (and hopefully, accurate) solution to any problem in which full credit was not awarded. The questions themselves should be written out as well (with problem numbers). Tests and quizzes and their accompanying corrections will be organized in a 3-hole file in the portfolio folder.

"Fixed" Entry #5

Contents Entry

This entry will most likely be completed last, yet it should be placed first in the Portfolio Entries. It must incude:

- **Table of Contents**
- **Scatterdiagram** depicting Entry Types and Methods (see below)
- **Letter to Reader** addressing, but not limited to, the following:
    - -Why were these topics chosen?
    - -What did you enjoy learning?
    - -What difficulties arose?
    - -Your reflections about this collection of portfolio entries
- **Work Log Sheet** (see below)

METHOD TYPES

In addition to being sure you have completed each of the required entries each quarter, you will also vary your methods as you complete your entries. For the most part, you may choose which entry types you will match up with which of the following methods. You don't have to use all the methods each quarter, but you must use all of them by the end of the third quarter. The methods include:

Making Use of Math-Related Software (or a Graphing Calculator)
Constructing Physical Models or Manipulatives
Working Without Peers (Individual Entry)
Working With Peers (Group or Pair Entry)

Using your Scatterdiagram, you are to keep track of the method for each of your entries.

WHAT OUTCOMES ARE EXPECTED?

What is immediately apparent in this math portfolio is what the expectations are for students. The seven "Points of Focus" (a wonderfully mathematical phrasing for "outcomes") present students with what is important right away. Whether a student feels competent to grapple with these concepts in September is not the concern. What is most important is that the student knows the expectations for June in September. What "type" of portfolio is this?

As noted earlier, most portfolios, in practice, are a hybrid of the best-works/selection/process categories, and the Heathwood Hall Math Portfolio is a wonderful example of just that. Heavily oriented toward the selection and process models, there is room, nonetheless, for some "best-work" by students and, indeed, there is an implicit expectation that the portfolio itself will ultimately be a "best-work."

This is also a good example of teacher-defined categories which students have varying degrees of choice over. It also includes a requirement for students to not only reflect on their work, but to explain choices that were made (in "fixed" Entry #5). So, while teachers have provided a carefully structured environment for students, with outcomes and assignments clearly delineated, there is still an inherent design element which demands that students be active, constructivist learners.

DEALING WITH THE GRADING ISSUE

Since it is the first year the Math Department at Heathwood Hall is implementing this portfolio, they have taken a wise step: the portfolio is worth 20% of each quarter's grade. In doing this, the portfolio assessment has not become an all-or-nothing, go-for-broke system. It allows the teachers to learn from it, to see what works best (this year) and what doesn't. By introducing it as a fraction of the course evaluation, students also have time to "learn the system." It may be that next year's portfolio will be worth 50% and that by the turn of the century the entire math program will be part of a portfolio system. What we can be sure of is that work done in math class will always have an eye toward the portfolio assessment, looking for connections and applicability.

GRADING PART 2: THE EVALUATION FORM

A later chapter will specifically address criteria, rubrics, evaluation, and performance assessment scoring, so the Evaluation Form from Heathwood Hall (Fig. 3.2) will not be analyzed in detail here. What is important to note about it, however, is that it exists! Consider how many tests, essays, or other evaluations students are subjected to where they have no idea what the expectation for excellent work is ("distinction" or "Honors") and must rely on some kind of psychic guessing about what a particular teacher's "standards" might be. That this mathematics department has included a rubric with its portfolio guidelines speaks to a significant issue which performance assessments address far more forthrightly than traditional methods of assessment. Rubrics and scoring will always raise issues of reliability and validity, however. Those issues are dealt with in the second volume of this book.

THE COURSE-LEVEL, UNIT PORTFOLIO

Can a Portfolio project serve the needs of a "curriculum-in-progress?" Can it be incorporated to meet the needs of "content coverage" while still developing a sense of student choice and permitting a teacher to push for both higher standards and "deeper" work? Figure 3.3 was used by the author in a Global Studies course at Bronxville High School in New York, and presents one way teachers may design a portfolio assessment to meet all the objectives described above. While "covering" a certain content area, it puts the responsibility of the work on the students, while requiring they engage in a multitasked assignment which ultimately demands higher-order critical thinking. Like Heathwood Hall's Math Portfolio, this assignment includes a scoring rubric (Fig. 3.4) which the students received *when they were given the assignment.* The importance of this step cannot be emphasized enough: if new assessments do not attempt to clarify what the expectation for quality work is, we are simply repackaging old wine in new bottles. Let's look at the assignment as the students received it and consider the possibilities and implications for classroom teachers initiating portfolio assessment in a similar fashion.

(Text continues on page 51.)

FIGURE 3.2: HEATHWOOD HALL
MATHEMATICS PORTFOLIO EVALUATION FORM

Non-Routine Puzzle

DISTINCTION
__ meets all 'honors' criteria
__ solution reflects inventive
   problem-solving
__ analysis of strategies used

HONORS
__ meets all 'competent'
   criteria
__ puzzle is challenging
__ solution is clearly
   communicated using
   appropriate notation
__ statement of strategies
   included

COMPETENT
__ student understands
   problem
__ puzzle is at least
   commensurate w/ability
__ problem successfully solved
__ problem is clearly
   communicated using
   appropriate notation

MARGINAL
__ student failed to
   understand problem
__ puzzle not commensurate
   w/ ability

comments_____

__ __ __ __ __ __ __ __
__ __ __ __ __ __ __ __
__ __ __ __ __ __ __ __
__ __ __ __ __ __ __ __
__ __ __ __ __ __ __ __
__ __ __ __ __ __ __ __
__ __ __ __ __ __ __ __
__ __ __ __ __ __ __ __
__ __ __ __ __ __ __ __
__ __ __ __ __ __ __

GRADE_____

Content Entry

DISTINCTION
__ meets all 'honors' criteria
__ overall portfolio exhibits
   clear enthusiasm in
   learning, progress in
   knowledge base, and
   healthy mathematical
   disposition

HONORS
__ meets all 'competent'
   criteria
__ overall protfolio exhibits
   pride in work and evidence
   of new learning

COMPETENT
__ all Content Entry
   components are present and
   in order
__ Letter to Reader
   thoughtfully addresses
   questions (as stated on p.?)
__ overall portfolio is
   generally organized and
   well-presented

MARGINAL
__ Content Entry incomplete
__ Letter to Reader lacks
   thoughtfulness
__ overall portfolio lacks
   organization or is poorly
   presented

comments_____

__ __ __ __ __ __ __ __
__ __ __ __ __ __ __ __
__ __ __ __ __ __ __ __
__ __ __ __ __ __ __ __
__ __ __ __ __ __ __ __
__ __ __ __ __ __ __ __
__ __ __ __ __ __ __ __
__ __ __ __ __ __ __ __
__ __ __ __ __ __ __ __
__ __ __ __ __ __ __

GRADE_____

Name_____

Portfolio Grade _____

Progress Entry
DISTINCTION
__meets all 'competent' criteria
__all corrections are neatly presented

COMPETENT
__all tests and quizzes included in order
__all corrections included as directed

GRADE_____

Application Entry
DISTINCTION
__meets all 'honors' criteria
__math content is challenging

HONORS
__meets all 'competent' criteria
__math content is substantive
__student investigates an example of math connection

COMPETENT
__math content is authentic
__connection to other subject is made clear

MARGINAL
__math content is trivial
__connection vague, if present at all

comments_____

_____
_____
_____
_____
_____
_____

GRADE_____

Math in Historical Context Entry
DISTINCTION
__meets all 'honors' criteria
__extentsive summary of math component

HONORS
__meets all 'competent' criteria
__thorough treatment of subject/multiple sources used
__essay is well-constructed
__message is well-informed

COMPETENT
__summary of math subject(s) included
__writing is grammatically correct
__message is coherent and accurate
__resources are used appropriately

MARGINAL
__inaccurate information
__message incoherent
__quality of resources inadequate

comments_____

_____
_____
_____
_____
_____
_____
_____
_____
_____
_____
_____

GRADE_____

Reading & Writing Entry
DISTINCTION
__meets all 'honors' criteria
__extensive exploration of examples or connections

HONORS
__meets all 'competent' criteria
__summary is well-constructed
__essay is challenging

COMPETENT
__original example(s) or connection included
__writing is grammatically correct
__summary is coherent and accurate
__essay is at least commensurate w/ability

MARGINAL
__original example(s) and connection missing
__summary incoherent
__student failed to understand essay
__essay not commensurate w/ability

comments_____

_____
_____
_____
_____
_____
_____
_____
_____
_____
_____
_____

GRADE_____

FIGURE 3.3: BRONXVILLE HIGH SCHOOL
GLOBAL STUDIES PORTFOLIO TASK

Global Studies Portfolio Task

• *Latin America* •

You have been appointed Assistant Undersecretary of State for Latin American Affairs. The Secretary of State wants a report on the specific country assigned to you, addressing the issues listed below. The Report is to be on his desk at 11:25 a.m., November 26th.

Report requirements: Background information according to the list below, and a clear, written response to the Essential Questions as Policy recommendations.

Background Information should include:

1. Demographics & other vital statistics

2. Historical Summary: Pre-Columbian, Colonial, Independence, Modern

3. Physical Survey

4. Economic Status: Labor, resources, trade, debt

5. Cultural Profile: art, religion, ethnic groups

6. Political & Social Conditions

7. Essential Questions: a) Even though most Latin American countries were founded at the same time as the United States, many have developed in vastly different ways. Explain how and why the country you have investigated has or has not developed along similar lines as the United States.

b) What are the prospects for this nation as it approaches the 21st century? What does it have or will it need for success in the future, based on your research and analysis?

c) What change in current American policy toward this nation would you recommend and why?

Finally: be prepared to present your information in class discussions, group work, and, possibly, in a formal debate setting..

FIGURE 3.4: BRONXVILLE HIGH SCHOOL
GLOBAL STUDIES PORTFOLIO CRITERIA

Global Studies
Latin America
Portfolio Criteria

_____

To receive an A on the portfolio project students would have to fulfil the following criteria:

1. **Demographics:** Must be clearly presented with explanations as to why the statistics chosen are significant. That is, statistics must have a purpose and should indicate to a reader some comparative signficance on a global scale.

2. **Historical Summary:** should be analytical in nature, focusing on major historical themes, events, and public figures as well as historical consistencies and inconsistencies which are still apparent in the nation today.

3. **Physical Survey:** Should clearly distinguish the unique physical characteristics of the nation studied -- accompanied by appropriate maps or charts reflecting those unique characteristics.

4. **Economics:** Should utilize historical information with current statistics to provide a long-range perspective on the nation's economics as well as providing an appropriate back-drop for the current economic status of the nation and its possible future endeavors.

5. **Cultural Profile:** Should reflect how some aspect of the nation's art distinguishes this nation as unique, while providing some clear background on the (Roman Catholic) Church's influence on the nation and region.

6. **Political and Social** analysis should, in a clear and sequential manner, present an accurate picture of the quality of life domestically, as well as the nation's position in international politics.

7. The essay answer to the **Essential Question** should, in Part One, use significant facts from U.S. and your Latin American nations' histories to clearly explain why the nations' have or have not developed similarly. In Part Two, speculation on the nation's 21st Century prospects should clearly focus those aspects of the country you consider most important for future success.

8. Finally: students would demonstrate --- in class discussions, individual discussions with the instructor, and in group activities --- a clear understanding of all aspects of the nation reported on in the portfolio, as illustrated through articulate explanation of problem-solving and clear, organized discussion on the nation's problems.

To receive a **B** on the portfolio project students would have to fulfil the following criteria:

1. **Demographics:** Must be clearly presented with some explanation as to why the statistics chosen are significant. That is, statistics must have a purpose and should indicate to a reader some signficance on a global scale.

2. **Historical Summary:** would focus on major historical themes, events, and public figures with some mention of historical consistencies and inconsistencies which are still apparent in the nation today.

3. **Physical Survey:** Identifies unique physical characteristics of the nation studied -- accompanied by an appropriate map or chart reflecting those unique characteristics.

4. **Economics:** Utilizes some historical information with current statistics to provide perspective on the nation's economics as well as providing some back-drop for the current economic status of the nation and its possible future endeavors.

5. **Cultural Profile:** Analyzes a work of art to present a unique aspect or perspective on the nation.

6. **Political and Social** analysis should present some perspective of the quality of life domestically, as well as the nation's position in international politics.

7. The essay answer to the **Essential Question** should make some accurate comparisons between U.S. and Latin American development which refelcts on each area's development AND should offer some ideas as to 21st Century prospects for the nation.

8. **Finally:** students would demonstrate --- in class discussions, individual discussions with the instructor, and in group activities --- an understanding of most aspects of the nation reported on in the portfolio, as illustrated through explanation of problem-solving and discussion of the nation's problems.

To receive a C on the portfolio project students would have to fulfil the following criteria:

1. **Demographics:** Students would present some statistics with explanations --- not necessarily in a clear or organized fashion to the reader.

2. **Historical Summary:** Focuses on some historical themes, events, and public figures as well as historical consistencies and inconsistencies which are still apparent in the nation today with little reflection or analysis.

3. **Physical Survey:** Identifies physical characteristics with minimal visual aids or explanations.

4. **Economics:** Discusses historical development of economics and current problems with little depth, insight or analysis, simply providing a "report" or a rephrasing from sources.

5. **Cultural Profile:** Reports on a work of art without strong analysis or connection to the culture. Neglects any clear reporting of the role of the Church in the culture.

6. Discusses **Political and Social** aspects with no clear or organized fashion which would provide the reader with insight or deeper understanding of the nation.

7. The essay answer to the **Essential Question** would attempt some comparison of U.S. and Latin American development and acknowledge 21st Century prospects without utilizing many facts or statistics effectively.

8.Student would demonstrate -- in class discussions, individual conferences with the instructor, and group activities --- some understanding of various characteristics reported on in the portfolio.

To receive a **D** on the portfolio project students would have to do the following criteria:

1. **Demographics:** Simply list a minimal number of statistics with no clear reasoning or explanation.

2. **Historical Summary:** Simply "report" on events in a weakly paraphrased manner, offering no analysis or insight or clear, original input.

3. **Physical Survey:** Simply list the physical characteristics of the nation, with no reasoning or analysis provided.

4. **Economics:** Provide a sketchy and unclear economic history or the nation with little or no perspective on current conditions and what those conditions mean in a global economy.

5. **Cultural Profile:** A straightforward and simplistic "report" on a work of art, providing no insight or analysis as to why the work is unique to the culture which created it.

6. **Political and Social** analysis would be minimal, barely describing the culture or providing any clear or distinguishing insights about the nation being studied.

7. The essay answer to the **Essential Question** would not clearly present the student's own, original ideas as to why the US and the Latin American nation have developed similarly or differently.

8. **Finally:** students would demonstrate --- in class discussions, individual discussions with the instructor, and in group activities --- little understanding of any of the aspects of the nation reported on in the portfolio.

To receive an **F** on the Portfolio Project a student would have to do minimal or NO work on HALF or more of the project and/or not turn the project in by the DEADLINE

WHAT ARE THE DESIRED OUTCOMES FOR THIS PORTFOLIO?

The need for students to develop fairly sophisticated research skills would be the most obvious outcome in this assignment. Since each student would only investigate one nation (rather than super-ficially examining two dozen), their research has a clear focus. The need to explore a variety of topics requires students to employ a number of media and resources (including people) to uncover the necessary information to write the required report. In essence, they are creating a foreign policy dossier on a Latin American country — an "authentic" task. That dossier, of course, is their portfolio and, in this case, each element of it "counts" toward a grade. In this fashion, a rather traditional assignment — a report on a foreign country — becomes a portfolio task for students.

That students must apply higher-order, critical thinking skills is another outcome which becomes apparent as we consider the assignment. Students have to discriminate which information is important and why it is significant enough to include. In that sense, the selection aspect of a portfolio assessment is introduced, and even though the category is teacher-defined (Economic Status, for example), students must make choices and select appropriate, or "defendable," information. Beyond that, the written report (for the Secretary of State) requires students to analyze, evaluate, and synthesize information — all higher-order, critical thinking skills. Good expository writing, of course, is another outcome for this task.

The trade-off for this "experiment," of course, is time. If we are to allow students the chance to really do research, to thoughtfully reflect on the information they uncover, to put that information together in a report they are proud of, then we have to allow for the time necessary to accomplish those ends. By dividing Latin America up, one country per student, for example, and letting the students pursue their research, simply "coaching" their progress and process, we may find that very little "extra" time is needed to complete such a project. And the outcomes and results are important enough for us to honestly reconsider the curriculum as it stands.

If we give a "Latin America" test 1 year later — a year after our course has ended — how will the students fare? Probably not very well if it's a multiple-choice, fact regurgitation test. Based on their portfolio task assignment, however, what could we honestly and fairly expect students *to be able to do* 1 year later? What if we gave the "Latin America" test and allowed the students an hour or two to search out some answers and report back what they had found? The point is a simple, yet important, one: with this approach students develop problemsolving and critical thinking skills that preparation for a one-shot test could never do. If we believe those are important outcomes, along with developing research and presentation skills, then the "time" trade-off becomes relatively insignificant in light of the deeper learning the students have internalized.

REFLECTIVE PRACTICE FOR TEACHERS

What is also learned, by the teacher in this case, is how effective this design is for students. In this particular case, the teacher had to ask if too many topics were required, detracting from the "depth" aspect of the assignment. In a future assignment, should the number of items be more limited and the reporting out facet of the project be more pronounced?

Another serious consideration for the teacher involves a change in work habits or work patterns. When developing performance assessments, teachers must "front-load" their tasks. That is, in an assignment like the Latin American Portfolio, consider what the teacher had to do *before the students ever saw the assignment*. The portfolio selection design, based on outcomes of significance, had to be determined. The librarian/media center would have to be consulted to determine if enough materials were available for students to do adequate research. Days and times in the library/media center would also have to be reserved. A scoring rubric would have to be designed, for student consideration and to heighten awareness of expectations. If necessary, the teacher might also want to assign certain Latin American countries to specific students, for any number of reasons — an ethnic background connection, a country which is less "complex" to research for a student with limited skills, and so on. Once that is all accomplished, *then* the teacher can present the assignment to the students and, from that point on, "coach" their progress. Unlike the traditional model, where the teacher is the primary worker in the classroom, performance assessments look for teachers to create and design curriculum and assessments which will demand the students become the workers during the class periods. To do this, however, requires forethought, preparation, and clear focus on performance outcomes for students long before anything happens in the classroom. This is why a simple portfolio task like the one described above, a task embedded in an existing curriculum framework, may be the wisest *first step* for practitioners considering using portfolios for assessment in their classrooms.

SCHOOLWIDE PORTFOLIO SYSTEMS

The Crefeld School, an independent institution in Philadelphia, and Central Park East Secondary School (CPESS), a public school in New York City, have both developed portfolio systems which are *required* for successful graduation from their schools. These ambitious and elaborate systems are designed to create an environment in which students must become very conscious of their learning from the moment they enter the school. While categories for portfolio inclusions are faculty-designed, with larger community input, the students are still responsible for selection and presentation of portfolio materials. There are certain similarities between the two systems, yet each is unique to its own setting, developing a portfolio requirement for evidence of student work and achievement which each school believes reflects the learning that should occur for students to receive a diploma. By examining each school's portfolio system we can analyze what the desired outcomes for the school's graduates are, and what is considered valuable and important for graduates of these schools to present clear evidence of — *before they can leave with diploma in hand!*

THE CREFELD SCHOOL PORTFOLIO EXHIBITION SYSTEM

Crefeld's system is straightforward, presenting students with six areas requiring completion before graduation. In each category, students are given examples of "successful" activities or papers, creating reference points as they begin to compile their portfolios. While examining Crefeld's Exhibition Portfolio (Fig. 3.5), remember to keep several questions in mind: what are the desired outcomes for students? What are the expectations and how do students know the standards?

(Text continues on page 62.)

FIGURE 3.5: THE CREFELD SCHOOL EXHIBITIONS PORTFOLIO

EXHIBITIONS PORTFOLIO - Exhibitions are created as a matter of course in the Crefeld Curriculum. The standards for evaluating competence are clearly defined by the teacher(s) evaluating the exhibition. Once the student can present a portfolio of exhibitions which demonstrate mastery in each one of the six categories described below, he or she will have satisfied the exhibition criteria for graduation. The portfolio can and should contain any other work which the student deems representative of his or her achievement. No single piece of work may qualify for more than one exhibition, but several exhibitions may relate and complement each other. It is expected that the student will complete all exhibitions by January of their Senior Year, otherwise plans for graduation will be reconsidered.

Exhibition #1 - Community Service / Leadership
Design and implement a project which has the following components:
1) A goal to provide a valuable, free service to the non-Crefeld community
     (local or larger). This service should help needy people, meet some
     social or community need, or improve the environment.
2) A plan which specifies time, date, location, people involved (at least 6),
     supplies needed and how those supplies will be obtained, organizational
     issues, activities involved, and methods for evaluating success.
3) An activity which implements the plan described above.
4) A formal presentation (written, oral, and/or audio-visual) which describes
     in detail the goal, the plan, and the activity, and which evaluates the
     effectiveness of the project (both product and process).

Examples of Successful Activities:
     Organizing a clean up of a park
     Collecting food or clothing for homeless people
     Organizing a group to work for a helping agency (ie. Action
          AIDS, a soup kitchen, Habitat for Humanity)
     Raising money for a helping organization through Car Washes,
          Bake Sales, etc.

<u>Exhibition Evaluation</u>
<u>Community Service / Leadership</u>

Committee Members: Mr. Patron/Rena/Rich
                        Student's Advisor

Design and implement a project which has the following components:

1) A goal to provide a valuable, free service to a specified community outside of
   Crefeld (local or larger). This service should help needy people, meet
   some social or community need, or improve the environment. Write
   your goal and discuss with advisor.

Advisor's Approval of Plan _____

Mr. Patron/Rena/Rich's Approval of Plan _____

2) A plan which specifies contact with the community being served, time, date,
   location, people involved (at least 6), supplies needed and how those
   supplies will be obtained, organizational issues, activities involved, and
   methods for evaluating success. Write out your plan and discuss with
   advisor.

Advisor's Approval of Plan _____

Mr. Patron/Rena/Rich's Approval of Plan _____

3) An activity which implements the plan described above.

Evidence of Activity (Video or Live)
        Advisor's Approval of Evidence _____

Mr. Patron/Rena/Rich's Approval of Evidence_____

4) A formal presentation (typewritten, oral, and/or audio-visual) which
   describes in detail the goal, the plan, and the activity, and which
   evaluates the effectiveness of the project (both product and process).

Presentation Must :
        a. be written, oral, and/or audio-visual _____
        b. describe in detail the goal, the plan, and the activity _____
        c. provide a reflective self-evaluation of process & product _____

Advisor's Final Approval _____

Mr. Patron/Rena/Rich's Approval of Plan _____

Exhibition #2 - Self-Reflection & Future Plan

Exhibition Evaluation
Self-Reflection & Future Plan

1) **Reflective Autobiography** (typewritten)

_____ Writing is technically correct.
_____ Standard essay-writing form is observed.
_____ Controlling image is clearly articulated, supported, and has poetic undertones.
_____ Content makes attempt to describe aspects of character and possible origins of characteristics.

English Teacher's Approval _____

2) **Formal Resumé** (typewritten)

_____ Standard resumé format observed.
_____ Appropriately complete and informative.
_____ Neatly & cleanly presented.

English Teacher's Approval _____

3) **Post-Graduation Plan** (college and/or job applications)

_____ Necessary applications collected, completed, and submitted.
_____ Necessary interviews completed.
_____ Plan is realistic and likely to succeed.

Advisor's Approval _____

4) **Personal Budget** (including sample tax forms)

_____ Budget accounts for all likely expenses.
_____ Budget and taxes are mathematically correct.
_____ Correct format used for budget and taxes.
_____ Budget is realistic and financially sound.
_____ Budget includes a computer spreadsheet.

Math Teacher's Approval _____

5) **Learning Styles Analysis**

_____ Addresses Classroom Learning.
_____ Addresses Reading & Writing Issues.
_____ Addresses Organization & Time Management.
_____ Addresses Study Habits.
_____ Addresses Independent Learning Situations.

Advisor's Approval _____

Advisor's Final Approval _____

Exhibition #3 - Study and Proposal
1) Identify some topic of concern to you and to the community (local or
      larger).
2) Plan some kind of original study which discovers new information about
      the issue.
3) Conduct the study using formal scientific and/or social science methods.
4) Prepare a formal report of the results and/or a proposal for some action or
      policy change based upon the results of your study.
5) Present your findings and/or proposal to some agency which has the power
      to implement your ideas (ie. governmental agency, board of directors,
      community group).

Examples of Successful Studies:
      Study water or air pollution in a community
      Conduct a survey of alums from a variety of schools to see how
            well they were prepared for life after high school
      Study the soil, sun, and climate of a property and make a
            landscaping plan
      Conduct a study of high school students to see how well
            informed they are about different topics (ie. AIDS, drugs,
            African-American history)

<u>Exhibition Evaluation</u>
<u>Study and Proposal</u>

Committee Members: Nick, Ari, Eric

1) Topic of concern has been identified as one that is of importance to a
   community.

Signatures _____   _____

2) Background research has been done to outline the current state of
   information on the topic. A hypothesis has been developed which
   requires the generation of new data for support.

Signatures _____   _____

3) A plan for a study has been devised which will adequately and fully test the
   hypothesis.

Signatures _____   _____

4) Study has been conducted in accordance with plan.

Signatures _____   _____

5) Formal report of study has been prepared and submitted (See rubric on back
   for detailed checklist).

Signatures _____   _____

6) Findings have been reported to a person or agency that has the power to
   utilize them in a way which benefits the community.

Signatures _____   _____

Exhibition #4 - Cultural Appreciation
1) Select a person, event, movement, or era which you feel has had a
     significant effect on your life and on society at large.
2) Study the topic using a diverse variety of primary and secondary sources.
     Become an expert on that topic.
3) Write a formal paper which demonstrates your mastery of the topic
     including your original interpretations and thoughts.

Examples of Successful Papers
          Alcoholics Anonymous
          Brown v. The Board of Education
          SAT Testing
          Bob Marley

Exhibition Evaluation
Cultural Appreciation

Committee Members: Rich
                          Ed
                          Jennifer
                          Tammy

1) Select a historical or famous person, event, movement, or era which you
     feel has had a significant effect on society at large or, through society,
     on your life.

Committee's Approval of Topic _____

2) Study the topic using a diverse variety of primary and secondary sources.
     Become an expert on that topic. Collect your sources in a bibliography
     and discuss with advisor.

Committee's Approval of Bibliography _____

3) Write a formal paper which demonstrates your mastery of the topic
     including your original interpretations and thoughts.

RUBRIC ON BACK
Committee's Approval of Report (based on rubric) _____

Exhibition #5 - Instruction
Engage in some instructional activity which includes lesson planning,
    instruction, and evaluation under the supervision of a professional
    educator. Some possible experiences include:
        a) Teaching Assistantship (course at Crefeld or elsewhere)
        b) Peer Tutoring (at least 30 hours with an individual)
        c) Teaching a unit in a class

Examples of Successful Activities
        Teaching a unit to a dance class
        Tutoring a student in math
        Being a teaching assistant for a course
        Teaching all seniors to make a budget on a spreadsheet

Exhibition Evaluation
Instruction

1. Statement of instructional activity and contact with mentor.

    Advisor's Approval of Situation _____

2. Sample lesson plan.

    Advisor's Approval of Plan _____

3. Evidence of Presentation (Video, Live, or Report from Mentor)

    Advisor's Approval of Evidence _____

4. Evidence of evaluation including self-evaluation and feedback from mentor.

    Advisor's Approval of Evidence _____

Exhibition #6 - Modes of Expression
The student must demonstrate some proficiency in a mode of expression other than written English prose. This proficiency should include at least two courses (or their equivalent) in the chosen mode of expression. The work must be presented for public appreciation. At least one professional from the field of your work must serve as a consultant and critique your work. Some possibilities include:
- an artistic portfolio
- a performance in a foreign language
- a collection of poetry
- an original computer program
- a performance of dance, music, and/or drama
- a construction project (design and implementation)
- an original lesson plan which you teach to a class (for
      teaching assistants only)

Examples of Successful Activities:
A portfolio of drawings and slides to use for art school
      admission
A computer program which solves quadratic equations
A dance performance
A lesson plan about the U.S. budget designed and taught by a
      teaching assistant
A play written and performed in Spanish

Exhibition Evaluation
Modes of Expression Exhibition

1. Student has planned and described the demonstration of proficiency sufficiently and obtained a commitment from a consultant who is a professional in the field (including name, qualifications, and phone number).

      Advisor's Approval of Situation _____

2. Student creates demonstration of proficiency.

3. Presentation of work. Evidence of Presentation (Video, Live, and/or Report from Mentor)

      Advisor's Approval of Evidence _____

4. Written reflection and/or formal discussion with evaluators on process and product including self-evaluation and feedback from consultant.

      Advisor's Approval of Reflection _____

WHAT ARE THE DESIRED OUTCOMES OF THE CREFELD SYSTEM?

By examining the six categories students must include in their portfolio, we are given a clear indication of what the valued outcomes of the school are. Community service, future planning, original independent study, cultural app reciation (broadly defined), the ability to teach others, and an ability to express oneself *beyond writing* are the required areas of inclusion. It should be noted that The Crefeld School requires students to pass competency tests in a variety of academic areas (math, science, language arts, social studies, etc.) *before* students are eligible to begin compiling their Graduation Portfolio. With that said, we can see that this portfolio presents a strong message about those values and skills students need *beyond* the traditional "walls" of the school. That the "portfolio can and should contain any other work which the student deems representative of his or her achievement" allows students to add a "Best Works" element to the Selection criteria.

EVALUATING THE PORTFOLIO

The committee system which accompanies each facet of the portfolio establishes guidelines and allows for personal shaping of criteria and standards for each portfolio item (Fig. 3.6). The close supervision is a significant aspect of this system and, as we have seen, is an important element of portfolio assessment, whether it's a class-level or schoolwide system. The need for advisor approval and careful planning by students is an integral part of each Crefeld portfolio. In certain cases — the Self-Reflection and Future Plan, as well as the Cultural Appreciation piece — a detailed rubric is presented to guide students through their process. Again, the interaction between students and teacher(s) is a most significant aspect of the portfolio. For portfolios to be a genuine learning experience, students not only need the ability to choose their directions but also require careful coaching and guidance as they navigate the process. Unlike many traditional "tests," portfolios do not operate on a *"gotcha"* premise — where testing is used to "catch" students not working. The philosophical foundation of portfolios is based on making students *responsible* for their learning, *investing* them in their work, and *coaching* them for success. The Crefeld portfolio system presents a design which includes all those elements.

A WORK IN PROGRESS

The Exhibitions Portfolio presented above was the 1993 version for Crefeld graduates and was the second year the school had conducted graduation-by-portfolio. It was different from 1992s design and the 1994 design included some changes from 1993's. 1995's will undoubtedly be different from 1994's. The point here is that performance assessments are always a work-in-progress for the faculty. By revisiting the assessment *after* the students have completed it, teachers can find out:

♦ What worked and what didn't?

♦ How can we make this even more effective for next year's group?

♦ Are there items we should change, omit, or add?

♦ Do our rubrics need to be more/less detailed?

By subjecting their own design and work to the same standards expected of the students, the portfolio system becomes a teaching/learning experience for *all* the members of the school community. Central Park East Secondary School has been working at their Graduation Portfolio for over 5 years. An examination of their work further reveals the benefits and potential of a schoolwide portfolio system.

CENTRAL PARK EAST SECONDARY SCHOOL: PORTFOLIO PIONEERS

As a Charter School in Theodore Sizer's Coalition of Essential Schools, Central Park East Secondary School has been the focus of much attention. Because of its location (East Harlem, New York City), its student population (ethnic minority "innercity" students), and its first Director (MacArthur Award winner Deborah Meier), it has been scrutinized and reported about in great detail over the last 5 years. The subject of a major film by Fred Wiseman (*High School*), a book by Seymour Fliegel (*Miracle in East Harlem*), numerous television shows and chapters in books, it might be thought that everyone knows all there is to know about CPESS. Nonetheless, it would be a disservice to the school and to any book dealing with performance assessments *not* to include the pioneering work this school has done. In fact, the Center for Collaborative Education

FIGURE 3.6: THE CREFELD SCHOOL—CULTURAL APPRECIATION EXHIBITION

CULTURAL APPRECIATION EXHIBITION EVALUATION

STUDENT -

DATE -

TITLE -

	None	Entry	Work	Comp	Excel
MECHANICS OF WRITING					
Correct spelling.					
Grammatically correct Standard English sentences.					
Chosen vocabulary is appropriate to situation.					
Tone & style of writing are appropriate for the purpose.					
Ideas are developed into coherent paragraphs.					
Writing has been improved through restructuring, correcting errors, and rewriting.					
STRUCTURE OF ESSAY					
Introduction clearly presents essay's ideas.					
Thesis statement is clearly identifiable.					
Each body paragraph performs an identifiable function.					
Topic sentences clearly relate paragraphs to thesis.					
Conclusion concisely summarizes essay's ideas.					

RESEARCH

An appropriate variety of primary and secondary sources are cited as evidence.

Data is used appropriately to support argument.

Quotes, paraphrases, and summaries are correctly used.

Footnotes are used properly.

Bibliography is in correct form.

REASONING

Questions are clearly identified and formulated.

Several answers to questions are proposed & evaluated.

Ideas are selected and related in an organized argument.

Facts and opinions are not confused.

Reasoning is sound and compelling.

Draws reasonable conclusions from information found in various sources.

CONTENT

Topic is appropriate for assignment.

Paper demonstrates adequate command of relevant data.

Facts presented are correct.

Conclusions reached are realistic.

PRESENTATION

Competently typed or word-processed.

Neatly and cleanly presented.

Standard academic paper form observed (cover, name, etc.)

in New York City has produced a videotape on *Graduation by Portfolio* which is a wonderful "warts-and-all" presentation of the struggles of implementing the system we examine here.

Central Park East has never backed away from the challenge of moving into unchartered waters — whether it's been interdisciplinary curriculum, extended teaching periods, or performance assessment. Their Graduation Portfolio system was one of the first genuine attempts to implement the Coalition of Essential School's principle of graduation by Exhibition, and the results have been impressive. CPESS graduates 99% of its students and 90% go on to 4-year colleges — a remarkable feat for an "innercity" school, indeed.

The Graduation Portfolio *is* the focus of the Junior and Senior years (The Senior Institute) at CPESS. It has elements which are similar to Crefeld's, as we will note, but it is a far more elaborate design, clearly geared at providing a strong academic background for its students. While examining the detailed description (Fig. 3.7) which follows, once again keep in mind the questions, "What are the desired outcomes for students?", and "How will they be evaluated toward those ends?"

THE OUTCOMES AND THE PORTFOLIO DESIGN

Far more than the Crefeld Portfolio, CPESS's system is geared toward being a cumulative presentation of student work and achievement. The sheer volume of this portfolio — with *14* items for inclusion — makes it a demanding, if not daunting, prospect for students. But, as with the other portfolios described earlier, the students know, right from the start, *what* the expectation is. Again, the clarity of the assignment regarding the categories (which are faculty/community designed) still allows for student choice, combining the aspects of selection, best-works, and process portfolios in a large-scale, multiyear project.

(Text continues on page 73.)

The Graduation Portfolio at
Central Park East Secondary School

GRADUATION REQUIREMENTS

In order to receive a diploma the student's Graduation Committee must attest to the fact that all of the following requirements have been met.

(1) An appropriate program of courses, seminars, independent study and internships has been completed during Division II and the Senior Institute that will meet the needs of their post-grad plan.

(2) The necessary NY State RCTs or their equivalent have been passed, and the student has demonstrated basic college entry-level skill in reading, writing and math.

(3) At least seven "major" Portfolio areas have been presented for a full Graduation Committee review and defense, and found at least satisfactory.

(4) All 14 Portfolio areas have been completed and accepted by the student's Graduation Committee.

(5) The Computing and Technology Expectations (see Appendix) have been met in the course of the regular Portfolios.

(6) A final Senior Project has been satisfactorily completed.

THE 14 PORTFOLIO AREAS: An Overview

The primary responsibility of the Senior Institute student is to complete the fourteen Portfolio requirements listed below.

These Portfolios reflect cumulative knowledge and skill in each area as well as the specific CPESS habits of mind and work. Students will present the work in all 14 Portfolio areas to their Graduation Committee for review and acceptance. They will meet for a full review on their seven "majors", to present, discuss and defend their work. There are therefore two stages to keep in mind - preparation of the Portfolio materials in collaboration with their Advisor and others, and then presentation and defense. In some cases Portfolio work will need to be expanded, modified and re-presented for final approval. Students may also choose to present work a second time to earn a higher assessment.

It is important to remember that a majority of the work done in connection with a Portfolio can and should be the outcome of the courses, seminars, internships and independent study that a student has engaged in during the normal course of his/her Senior Institute years. In addition, some of the material may be an outgrowth of work initiated in Divisions I or II, or where appropriate even work completed prior to entering the Senior Institute.

Portfolios include work in fourteen areas: seven "majors" and seven "others." There is no one way to complete these requirements, nor one way to present them. Just as individuals are different, the individual Portfolios will reflect these differences. A Portfolio is a term covering all the ways in which a student exhibits his/her knowledge, understanding and skill.

For example, work completed to meet one requirement can be used to fulfill other requirements as well. CPESS recommends intradisciplinary studies wherever possible. While the final review will be based on individual accomplishment, almost all Portfolio requirements can be based on work done in collaboration with others as well as group presentations. Such collaborative work is encouraged, since it often enables a student to engage in a much more complex and interesting project.

Quality and depth of understanding, the good use of CPESS" five "habits of mind", and the capacity to present convincing evidence of mastery as relevant to each particular field are the major criteria used by the Committee. However, Portfolio work must reflect a concern for both substance and style. For example, written work must be submitted in clear, grammatical English that reflects the expected proficiency level of a high school graduate re spelling, grammatical errors and legibility. Errors should be eliminated before the Portfolio is presented to the Committee. (Written work must generally be submitted in typewritten form, for example.)   The same care in preparation and presentation applies to all other forms of work. Portfolio work should represent a student's best effort. The same holds true for the manner of presentation.

Different characteristics are more or less relevant to each Portfolio area. Each academic discipline, for example, has developed its own "scoring grid" to help students and Graduation Committee members focus objectively on the appropriate criteria. Over time the criteria for acceptable performance will be more fully developed - both through the creation of more such "grids" as well as through the compilation of past student work that demonstrates accepted levels of skill. Students are expected to become familiar with the criteria by which they are measured, both the scoring grids and former student work.

The following are the 14 Portfolio areas:

1. Post Graduate Plan:

2. Science/Technology*

3. Mathematics*

4. History*

5. Literature*

6.   Autobiography

7.   School and Community Service and Internship

8.   Ethics and Societal Issues

9.   Fine Arts/Aesthetics

10. Practical Skills & Knowledge

11. Media

12. Geography

13. Language Other Than English

14. Physical Challenge

Senior Project: One of the above Portfolio topics or items will be separately assessed as a final Senior project.

Each student is required to make a major presentation in seven of the 14 areas described above.   These include the four starred Portfolios, and at least 3 others chosen in cooperation with his/her Advisor.   Grades of Distinguished, SatPlus, Sat or MinSat will be used to grade work presented as part of the Portfolio, as well as for the Portfolio area as a whole.   In the seven "minor" Portfolio areas, a student may choose a pass/fail grade.   Permission to do so, however, must be arrived at in consultation with his/her Advisor.

Senior Institute Portfolio Requirements

Graduation from CPESS is dependent upon completion of a Portfolio. Courses, seminars and independent study are the means by which students develop the skills and knowledge to complete the Portfolio. Portfolios include work in 14 required areas. There is, however, no one way to complete these requirements. Just as individuals are different, so the individual Portfolios reflect such differences. Work completed to meet one Portfolio can be used to fulfill other requirements. The following represents a brief outline of each Portfolio requirement.

1. Post-Graduation Plan
This plan outlines the purpose for earning a high school diploma. It includes short-range goals, such as getting into college or a particular job-training program. It also includes longer-range life and career ambitions.

2. Autobiography
The autobiography includes key events and people that have influenced a student's development.

3. Internship
A semester-long internship/apprenticeship in a chosen career field is required. Students then present an assessment of what they gained from the job experience in terms of skills, knowledge and attitudes.

4. Ethics, Social Issues & Philosophy
The ability to engage in moral reasoning and to support one's ethical views is the aim of this Portfolio. The topics can be personal moral choices or contemporary political/social issues.

5. Literature
An essay is required that demonstrates literary reflectiveness and the capacity to communicate ideas in written form. Students submit at least one piece of written work about an individual book, author or collection of books/authors.

Students also prepare an Annotated Bibliography of novels, plays and poetry that they have read during their high school years and which they are prepared to discuss.

Students must pass the New York State Regents Competency Test in Writing and the CUNY Freshman Placement Test in Writing and Reading.

6. History
Students must demonstrate a capacity to work as an historian. Students select a particular historical problem, issue or event to investigate, do research with primary and secondary documents, weigh evidence, compare conflicting views and make comparisons and predictions.

Students also prepare a time-line of major events in world and U.S. history that they have studied during their high school years.

Students must pass the Regents Competency Test in U.S. History and Government.

7. Geography

Students must demonstrate an ability to use maps and globes, locate major physical and political divisions, pass a short-answer quiz and exhibit more specialized knowledge of one field of geography.

8. Second/Third Language

Students must demonstrate competence in four areas of language acquisition in a language other than English: speaking, listening, reading and writing. Students take a minimum of five semesters of language instruction and/or pass the New York State language proficiency test. Students must defend the importance of their second/third language experience to their Graduation Committee.

9. Mathematics

Formal competence in math is demonstrated by passing the Regents Competency Test and the City University of New York Freshman Placement Test.

Students exhibit a more in-depth understanding of math by choosing one specific area to explore and apply to real-life circumstances; for example, statistics or mathematical models.

10. Science & Technology

Familiarity with a wide range of terms and issues throughout the sciences is assessed through the Regents Competency Test.

Students also choose one topic in any of the sciences and must exhibit their knowledge of this in a manner consistent with scientific presentations.

11. Fine Arts & Aesthetics

Students must offer evidence of talent and experience and/or knowledge and understanding in one of the fine arts - visual arts, music, drama, poetry, dance. Evidence may involve a public exhibition or performance.

12. Mass Media

Students must show an awareness of the impact of the mass media on society. This may take the form of a dialogue on the role of advertising, or film criticism, or even the production and editing of a video or other media form.

13. Practical Skills & Know-How

Students must demonstrate a wide range of everyday-life skills needed to function and contribute to society. These proficiencies include an understanding of issues of health, sex, family care, drug and substance abuse, the use of appliances (automobiles, computers) and issues of personal economics and citizenship (voter registration).

14. Physical Challenge

Students present evidence of proficiency in at least one sport or physical activity and demonstrate an understanding of the benefits of a healthy lifestyle.

Like Crefeld, we can see CPESS's concern that students clearly prepare for the world beyond their walls, requiring an autobiography and a postgraduate plan. And, like Crefeld, there is a definite value placed on contributing to the community — in this case through service or an internship. The inclusion of a "Practical Daily Skills and Know-How" combined with "Health and Lifetime Fitness Education" adds a component which makes a clear statement to students as to what the school and community think will be essentials for the world beyond CPESS.

Yet, the CPESS Portfolio carefully addresses the intellectual and academic life of its students, too. Philosophy, Mathematics, Fine Arts, Geography, Media, Science, Literature, and History provide a rigorous view of curriculum by any standard. What is important to note here, in examining the design of portfolios, is *what* is included, *how much* latitude students have in their choices, and *how* will the work be evaluated? While it was mentioned that students have choice in compiling their portfolio, there are several explicit messages about the expected quality of work. The one scoring guide (Fig. 3.8) included reflects the breadth and depth of work students need to attain to "pass," much less achieve any designation of "distinguished" work.

The *tone* of the description of the CPESS Portfolio reflects a great deal about how the faculty and students see this endeavor. The importance of each category, the detail with which it is presented, the rationales which are offered, once again point to the "front-loading" work staff must put into its development of a portfolio system. Consider, too, how, knowing these are the portfolio guidelines *for graduation*, faculty must scrutinize and examine its curricular offerings each semester! There is no room here for frivolous electives or tangential topics which some teacher happens to be passionate about. By the time students reach the Senior Institute, work *must* become focused on the portfolio — for both students and teachers.

A NOTE ON PROCESS AND EVALUATION

It should be understood that students can begin bringing their portfolios before the appropriate committees as soon as they enter the Senior Institute. Unlike traditional systems in which Final Exams

FIGURE 3.8: CENTRAL PARK EAST SECONDARY SCHOOL
SCORING GUIDE: MATHEMATICS AND SCIENCE

	View Point	Connections
	Encompasses Wide Knowledge Base but Is Focussed	**The Whole Is Greater than the Sum of the Parts**
	• Clearly identifies, addresses key question & idea; • Demonstrates an in-depth understanding of the issues; • Presents position persuasively and discusses other views when appropriate.	• Explain significance of problems/issues beyond the project; • Conjectures, Predicts, and explains observations where appropriate; • Organized so that all parts support the whole; • Contains useful transitions; • Concludes in a satisfying way.
E X C E E D S	Paper is highly focussed showing good depth of understanding and good breadth.	All parts support the whole and make connections beyond the scope of the paper.
M E E T S	Paper is focussed with depth and some breadth.	Most parts support the whole, resulting in a paper more significant than the information provided in the parts.
A P P R O A C H	Focus is inconsistent, making it difficult to evaluate the depth and breadth of understanding.	Connections of parts to the whole are sometimes made.
N E E D S	Lacks focus and direction.	Not yet able to connect the parts to the whole.

Comments:

Evidence	Voice	Conventions
Credible/Convincing • Generalizations & ideas supported by specific relevant and accurate information, which is developed in appropriate depth; • Contains discussion of strengths and weaknesses of evidence; • Cites appropriate resources; • Uses graphs, formulas, figures, and equations accurately.	**Engaging** • Lively, interesting use of language; • Awareness of reader (explains concepts so they are understandable to the lay person); • Student uses own language[.]	**Legible and Intelligible** • Excellent appearance; • Correct format; • Varied sentence structure; • Good mechanics and standard notation; • Appropriate, broad vocabulary and word usage.
Paper is very convincing.	Paper is very captivating.	Excellent use of conventions.
Paper may be lacking in some of the qualities above, but retains credibility.	Appropriate language, style and tone chosen.	Paper has a minimal number of errors which do not interfere with understanding.
Paper includes some evidence relevant to the topic, but lacks enough of the above qualities to diminish credibility.	Shows some awareness of reader and attempts to inform, but language, style, or tone is confused.	Paper contains errors which minimally interfere with understanding.
Paper contains little specific evidence relevant to the topic.	Paper lacks awareness of reader and adopts no particular language, style, or tone.	Poor use of conventions interferes with understanding of the paper.

become the all-or-nothing determinant of student success or progress, the portfolio system is, by design, aimed at self-correction and success. If that means a student has to do an additional semester of work to graduate, that is a consequence which has to be clear — expectations and standards cannot be adjusted for the "social" promotion of students who are not prepared to graduate.

And this is where portfolios and performance assessments distinguish themselves from traditional tests and evaluation instruments. Looking at a system like Central Park East's, or Crefeld's, we can see, in terms of tangible evidence, what students know and are able to do. Their diplomas are *not* simply certificates which reflect "time spent" at the institution. If our goal is, in fact, making sure students leave our schools with skills and knowledge, no "national curriculum" or "national test" could ever prove that more powerfully than the kind of portfolio systems CPESS and the Crefeld School are developing. And, while these may not be perfect systems, they clearly provide students, parents, faculty, and the community at large with significant and tangible evidence of student achievement and progress.

Is it possible, then, to create portfolios above the classroom or schoolwide levels? What would the positive reasons for developing a statewide portfolio system be? What would the drawbacks be? Would such a system, if it worked, provide a model for a National Portfolio System (a new Goals 2000 objective, perhaps)? We can answer these questions by examining a state which has attempted to implement a statewide portfolio systems, Vermont. The early work and results should prove instructive to anyone interested in the design and implementation of performance assessments — and particularly regarding portfolio assessment even at the classroom level.

A STATEWIDE PORTFOLIO SYSTEM

The Vermont statewide portfolio system has come under fire in its first years of existence. This is understandable, given the radical departure this assessment system represents from the established norms. What should also be understood, however, is that a system like this require time to be developed and, as mentioned earlier, will always have an aspect of a work-in-progress about it. The problems arise on several fronts when implementing a statewide system, though, and Vermont provides valuable lessons for us.

How will individual district or school assessments be affected by a statewide system? How will evaluation of such programs be conducted, and who, ultimately, is responsible for improving student achievement? We have seen the problems which arise from questions such as these. The fact that these are hard questions and that performance assessments are "messy" systems to implement, though, should not cause the work to stop. A problem anyone will face when starting down the performance assessment path is that this work takes time and, in a culture which too often requires immediate results (and usually in a simplistic, quantified score), the pressure to produce "results" will compete with the development of an authentic system which reflects genuine student achievement. Certainly the brouhaha following the scoring of the first Language Arts Portfolios in Vermont is evidence of this.

Statewide portfolio systems raise the same issues any portfolio assessment will encounter — it's simply on a grander scale. Developing rater and inter-rater reliability is always a problem when "scoring" any kind of writing or problemsolving work by students. The vast improvement in the Math Portfolio scoring in Vermont's second year speaks to the work-in-progress aspect of this kind of system and, while the Language Arts program still faced difficulties, improvement was shown there, too.

What's important to focus on in looking at the Vermont system, though, is what we can learn about portfolio assessment. How can we adapt the ideas and concepts presented in this system to improve our own portfolio system development? What strikes us as important or valuable in these systems which might benefit our system? What can we learn from its design and experience which may be worth bringing to the attention of policymakers in our own states, should we be called upon to recommend the values of performance assessments at that level? These are the questions worth focusing on as we examine the first statewide portfolio systems developed in the 1990s.

In looking at Vermont's portfolio assessments, several points should be made. The system was initiated with 4th and 8th graders, with 10th and 12th grade to be added successively. The basic design format would remain the same, however, so those early examples are the ones presented here. Vermont's system includes Language Arts *and* Mathematics (Fig. 3.9) — an ambitious undertaking, without a doubt. A significant component, which one can see in the broad outline design, is for individual schools to use the portfolio assessment to gauge the quality of their own program. Typically, performance assessments are *not* simply for viewing student work. An important aspect of performance assessments, and the Vermont system speaks to this, is that the progress of student work should be revealing to the school itself, as feedback on the effectiveness of its curriculum and instruction. So, while we collect and analyze student work, there is an important subtext which addresses the *quality* of the programs which produce the student work. By examining the Vermont portfolio guidelines we can see how the system is designed to assess student, teacher, and school district work.

(Text continues on page 82.)

FIGURE 3.9: VERMONT'S LANGUAGE ARTS AND MATHEMATICS PORTFOLIOS

Language Arts Portfolio Assessment

Items included:

table of contents	a dated "best piece"
dated letter from the student to the reviewers explaining the choice of the "best piece, as well as the process of writing it	a dated personal response to a cultural, media, or sports event; or to a book, current event, math problem, or science concept
a dated poem, short story, play, or personal narration	3 dated prose pieces from any subject area *other than* English or Language Arts

Assessment Criteria

Five dimensions of writing are to be rated on the following levels of performance: extensively, frequently, sometimes, rarely

♦ *Purpose* — Does writer: establish & maintain a clear purpose; Demonstrate awareness of audience & task; Exhibit clarity of ideas

♦ *Organization* — Does the writer's response illustrate unity coherence

♦ *Details* — To what degree are the details appropriate for the writer's purpose and support the writer's main point?

♦ *Voice/Tone*— Does the response reflect personal investment and expression

♦ *Usage, mechanics, grammar* — Does the writer use correct usage (word choice, tense formation, agreement), mechanics (spelling, capitalization, punctuation), grammar; sentences

Reviewers were asked to respond to three questions about the school's program:

♦ Is there progress from earlier dated works to more recent works?

♦ Is there evidence of variety which will challenge all students and allow for an opportunity for success?

♦ Is there evidence of teacher/peer response to student drafts, and opportunity for students to revise?

Mathematics Portfolio

Included items:

♦   By year's end, portfolios should contain 10–20 entries.

♦   5–7 pieces should be "best pieces," selected by students and teachers — among which there should be

   •   response to a logic/mathematical puzzle or word problem
   •   complex investigation of a topic, with data collection and research; may be short- or long-term project
   •   evidence of group work as well as individual work

♦   A "letter to the evaluator" explaining the rationale for works included.

Criteria

Seven general categories were selected, with four choices for ratings in each category.

1.   *Understanding of task* — Explanation of task, reasonableness of approach, correctness of response leading to inference of understanding
    (Ratings: 1.totally, 2. partially, 3. understood, 4. generalized, applied, extended)

2.   *Quality of Approaches/Procedures (How)* — demonstrations, descriptions, drafts, scratch work, etc.
    (Ratings: 1. inappropriate, 2. appropriate some of the time; 3. workable approach/procedure; 4. efficient or sophisticated approach)

3.   *Decisions along the way (Why)* — Changes in approach, explanations, demonstration
    (Ratings: 1. no evidence; 2. reasoned decisionmaking possible; 3. reasoned decisionmaking inferred with certainly; 4. reasoned decisionmaking explained)

4.   *Outcomes of Activities (What)* — Solutions; extension — observations, connections, applications, generalizations, synthesis, abstractions
    (Ratings: 1. solution without extensions; 2. solutions with observations; 3. solution with connections or application; 4. solution with synthesis, generalization, abstraction)

5.   *Language of Mathematics* — Terminology; notations, symbols
    (Ratings: 1. no or inappropriate use of math language; 2. appropriate use some of the time; 3. appropriate use most of the time; 4. use of rich, precise, elegant, appropriate math language)

6. *Mathematical Representations* — Graphs, tables, charts, models, diagrams, manipulatives
    (Ratings: 1. no use of math representations; 2. use of math representations; 3. accurate and appropriate use of math representations; 4. perceptive use of math representations)

7. *Clarity of Presentation* — Audio/video tapes or transcripts; written work; teacher interviews/observations; journal entries; student comments on cover sheet; student self-assessment
    (Ratings: 1. unclear (disorganized, incomplete, etc.); 2. some clear parts; 3. mostly clear; 4. clear (well-organized, complete, detailed))

Also included were "Empowerment Comments" regarding:

- Motivation
- Risk-taking
- Confidence
- Curiosity/interest
- Flexibility
- Reflection
- Perseverance
- Values math

Content area considerations include:

- Number sense
- Estimation
- Algebra
- Measurement
- Operations/place value
- Patterns/functions
- Geometry/spatial sense
- Statistics/probability

WHAT OUTCOMES DO THE VERMONT PORTFOLIOS ADDRESS?

We can see that the Language Arts Portfolio is designed to look at a breadth of student writing over time, with an eye toward process. It includes elements of selection and best-work, too, and requires student and teacher involvement at all levels. What is very clear in the Vermont design is a consciousness of *audience* in writing, from its table of contents to its "letter to the reviewer," as well as its selected pieces. The criteria, which are problematic due to their language, nonetheless delineate those aspects of writing which are valued: clarity, mechanics, purpose, personal expression. If seen as a guideline for developing schoolwide or classroom writing, then, the Vermont Language Arts Portfolio sets the parameters and broad goals for such a system. If a teacher, school, or district uses the state-wide system as its outline, the goals for writers throughout their academic career are delineated. The levels at which students achieve these goals is, of course, another matter, and this is where the Vermont system is still a work-in-progress. Again, as will be discussed later, the creation of benchmark performances which meet criteria is in a developmental stage in performance assessments and should not be seen as a mark of "failure" in its early phases. We have clearly seen in the past that multiple-choice tests on mechanics and usage are certainly no guarantee that students will learn to write. The Vermont Language Arts Portfolio is an attempt at developing a design which genuinely *teaches* writing as part of a curriculum and assessment system.

In much the same way, the Mathematics Portfolio is aimed at focusing on those aspects of *learning* mathematics which will enable students to actually *use and understand* the patterns of mathematical thought, and not simply see the discipline as one which requires "plug-in" algorithms and formulae. Despite the complicated rating system, the criteria for scoring student work does inform the class-room practitioner as to *what* valued outcomes the state of Vermont is focused on. Understanding a task at hand, breaking down the "why," "what," and "how" of problem solving in clear mathematical language and with mathematical representations, are all goals for this system. By also including content areas and "empowerment" comments, the goals are further clarified for both teachers and students. Again, the degree of difficulty of problems, as well as sophistication of solutions, is not clearly represented in the criteria and much is left to individual teachers, schools, and districts to develop along those lines. But this again speaks to the system as a work-in-progress and should serve to further the work of anyone designing portfolio assessments. The work which is out *in the field*, which has already been done in places like Vermont, should serve as guideposts for the *next generation* of performance assessments.

PORTFOLIO ASSESSMENT:
WHAT DO WE KNOW AND WHAT CAN WE LEARN?

We have seen that portfolios come in a variety of styles and designs. There is no "one way" to "do" portfolios — their design should be based on what kind of feedback which is most important for students and teachers to acquire for improved performance. Therefore, whether it's selection, best works, or process (or some combination), the portfolio must be thoughtfully designed to insure progressively better work by students, while providing teachers with a growing database informing them of the effectiveness of curriculum and instruction. In each of the examples presented here, the search for *outcomes* has been the primary task, for in determining *what* we expect from students we can begin to determine *how* and *why* those outcomes are, in fact, valued or significant. In all cases, the focus on *thoughtful* and *purposeful* design based on outcomes promoting student growth and progress over time has been paramount.

Published rubrics and/or criteria are features which appear throughout the examples presented in this chapter. It is important to see these as integral to the design of not only portfolio assessments, but to any performance assessments. Scoring rubrics and criteria more fully describe the outcomes and expectations the assessments are developed to achieve. These can be particularly problematic aspects for the novice assessment designer — we have no history of teachers carefully developing scoring rubrics. Because schools have operated through external testing — whether by standardized tests or "canned" textbook exams — the question has never been called: *What are the standards and criteria in this (classroom/ district/state)?* If a test or quiz wasn't gauged on a 100-point scale, how was a student to know what an "A" or a "B" or a "C" *really* represented? Was the "B" from one teacher in the Social Studies

Department *worth the same* as from another teacher in the same Department? In other words, what *were* the standards and criteria by which student work was being judged? The publication of rubrics and criteria in conjunction with these assessments *at the very least* allows for conversations and conferences between students and teachers regarding the work at hand. So, imperfect as this first generation of rubrics and criteria may appear at first glance — *consider the alternative!* And for that, alone, the move toward performance assessments takes on significance for students, teachers, parents, and the community: the conversation about standards *has to* emerge when these assessments appear.

Developing reliable, valid, and effective rubrics, criteria, and standards are all significant issues which are discussed in a later chapter. What is relevant to this chapter is that the examples presented go to great lengths to elucidate what the designers believe *quality work* consists of. And they try, at the very least, to express their ideas in rubrics which students have access to! This raises another important issue connected to portfolio assessments: the high level of student participation, input, and involvement in the process. Every step of the way, the student must be an *active* partner in creating, developing, *and assessing* the portfolio. In cases like the Crefeld School or Central Park East it is essential for students to be totally committed to working on the portfolio because it *is* their graduation requirement. The other examples also require a high level of student involvement, and this characteristic of portfolio assessment is a design feature which is *as important* as the outcomes and expectations articulated for the assessment.

Briefly put, then, key design elements to consider when developing portfolios are:

♦ Specifying valued/desired outcomes and expectations;

♦ Creating rubrics and criteria which define quality work; and

♦ Active student participation in the creation and development of the portfolio.

That the portfolio will include a variety of student work, often collected over a designated period of time, goes without saying. Certainly this is what "active student participation" would be. So, while portfolios reflect the students, school, or district where they are developed, there are certain elements which are fundamental to make the design most effective.

As a final note, it should be mentioned one last time that this is an arduous process which includes a roller coaster ride of highs and lows for the teachers and students involved. It is never easy to be among the first to venture into new territory. The examples in this chapter are intended to encourage others to embark on their own paths of performance assessment design. This sampling presents some of the early guideposts down these new roads. The hope is that they will serve to encourage, provide ideas, and be a kind of "launch pad" for the next generation of performance assessments which will move students into the 21st century. And, like a portfolio itself, the reader is asked to pick and choose those items in the chapter which seem significant, important, exciting, or provocative — and *use* them in the creation of newer and better portfolio systems. The important element in performance assessment development is that it is constantly "under construction," and anyone can join the crew and push the work further.

4

SOCRATIC SEMINARS: DISCUSSIONS WITH A DIFFERENCE

It is not uncommon for teachers, no matter what the discipline area they work in, to consider "class participation" or "class discussions" as part of student grades. And if we want students to learn to reason effectively and present evidence for their points of view, this is an appropriate area of accountability. But how rigorous are these discussions and on what criteria are they judged? Too often, a "class participation" grade is based on subjective impressions a teacher has of his or her students. How many teachers have accurate documentation of student participation in discussions? And, if we are going to focus on the idea of student-active, student-centered work, how much student-to-student discussion is engendered in classrooms?

The answers to these questions, if not self-evident, are known to anyone who has observed classes in secondary schools. Little accurate documentation is kept regarding student participation — and even less regarding the *quality* of student participation in classes. Moreover, most classroom discussions operate like a bicycle wheel, with the teacher as the hub. In essence, class "discussions" are a series of dialogues in which the teacher invariably makes every other comment. While this may be appropriate in some instances, the question which has to be raised is, "How can we promote greater student-to-student interaction in discussions of substance, and how can that activity serve as an authentic assessment of student progress in critical thinking and public speaking skills?" One answer to that question is Socratic Seminars.

Socratic Seminars are the product of the work of Mortimer Adler, the Director of the Institute for Philosophical Research in Chicago. With the publication of *The Paideia Proposal* in 1982 and *Paideia Problems and Possibilities* in 1983, Adler presented "An Educational Manifesto" designed to restructure how school was presented to students. Firmly rooted in the progressive tenets of John Dewey, Adler contended that the same course of study should be presented to *all* students, from age 4 through graduation from secondary school. Further, that education should be fundamentally rooted in three goals: "the acquisition of knowledge," the "development of intellectual skills (the skills of learning)," and the "enlarged understanding of ideas and values." In Adler's view, the first goal was delivered through didactic teaching, the use of textbooks, and "covered" content areas. The second goal was developed through "coaching, exercises, and supervised practice" in the skills areas of reading, writing, speaking, listening, calculating, problemsolving, and so on. The final goal was to be achieved through "Socratic Questioning and Active Participation," using books (*not* textbooks) and other works of art, as well as through "involvement in artistic activities" (all quotes from *The Paideia Proposal*, p. 23). According to Adler's proposal, the ultimate goal of schooling was to prepare all students to succeed in the third goal area.

He clearly notes that "these three kinds of learning and teaching cannot take place effectively in the same kinds of classrooms . . ." (p. 53), and makes an early case for restructuring schools around outcomes of significance. Pointing out that " The ordinary classroom, with students sitting in rows and the teacher standing in front, dominating it, . . . for fifty minutes, properly serve the purposes of didactic instruction, but nothing else" (p. 53), Adler goes on to make a compelling case for instituting student seminars which are based on a Socratic model. An important distinction here is that Adler is *not* making a case for a *Socratic questioning style,* which many teachers already employ. That would simply produce the "bicycle spokes" model described earlier and would be used as part of a didactic style, according to *The Paideia Proposal.*

The Socratic Seminar Adler proposes is one which is started with a teacher's question, to be sure, but the entire context of the learning environment is changed.

> Teaching by discussion imposes still other requirements. For older children, it calls for more than a fifty-minute class period. It also calls for a room in which the participants in the discussion sit around a table instead of in rows. The teacher is one of the participants, not the principal performer standing up in front of the group.
>
> The teacher's role in discussion is to keep it going along fruitful lines — by moderating, guiding, correcting, leading, and arguing like one more *student!* The teacher is first among equals. All must have the sense that they are participating as equals, as is the case in a genuine conversation.
>
> *The Paideia Proposal,* p. 54

Yet this is more than simple conversation, because there is a distinct focus to the discussion, and that focus is a text — be it a book, painting, film clip, mathematic theorem, scientific proposition, newspaper editorial, whatever.

The Socratic Seminar is *not* a "class discussion." Examining Adler's proposal carefully, considering how it needs to be implemented, its value as an performance assessment emerges. Dennis Gray, an original member of *The Paideia Group* and then Deputy Director of the Council for Basic Education, has become the foremost proponent and teacher-trainer in the Socratic Seminar method and, as such, has produced a wealth of material to help teachers better understand the practice. Based on Adler's concepts, Gray has designed a series of workshops (and, over the years, trained others to lead such workshops) which actively engage participants in Socratic Seminars, concurrently teaching effective seminar leadership.

An integral component to the training is that teachers who aspire to lead Socratic Seminars *must* participate in them first. This is also in keeping with Adler's precept that "teachers should be *on the way* to becoming educated persons" (*The Paideia Proposal*, p. 58). The need for active participation is mentioned here because this is a discussion of Socratic Seminars as a form of performance assessment and should *not be read as a substitute* for learning about leading seminars. That can only occur *through participation*! So, while portions of this chapter will refer to Dennis Gray's materials and methods, the intention here is to make people *aware* of Socratic Seminars, expose readers to examples of those already using seminars, and make a strong case for more teachers receiving training in this method *because* of its value as an performance assessment tool.

How it Works

As with all the performance assessments discussed thus far, Socratic Seminars start with *outcomes*. Clearly focusing on what it is students should know and be able to do *during* and *after* the seminar is the first step in the design process. What makes this particular form of assessment valuable is the variety of *outcomes* which can be achieved through its use — offering the assessment designer the opportunity to use this method of instruction any number of times. In fact, Adler makes a case for instituting at least 1 day each week in which *all* students participate in seminar. Some schools have done just that, while others leave it to the discretion of individual teachers or teams of teachers. The significant note to be taken here is that Socratic Seminar should be a recurring practice in a classroom or a school. It is an effective performance assessment because of the numerous *outcomes* it can address, thereby creating a consistent method for achieving diverse goals.

An array of critical thinking skills can be approached through the seminar method — analysis of text, synthesis of ideas, evaluation of concepts, inferential reasoning, etc. The seminar can also be used to rigorously develop reading comprehension skills — comprehension exhibited through application, analysis, and so on. It is also a method for developing speaking and listening skills. Because it occurs with frequency, even the most shy students will begin to contribute — particularly when the focus-text is one which deeply engages them.

Socratic Seminars invariably include a written component. No Socratic discussion is really complete without students writing about the ideas presented or the quality of the seminar itself (Did everyone participate? What was the *quality* of individual comments — were insights rendered? What new ideas were revealed in the seminar?) So, a variety of writing skills are another set of outcomes this method can address.

Once an outcome or set of outcomes is decided, teachers can survey the possible "texts" they might use. Here, again, we see how performance assessments are embedded in curriculum and instruction. The pedagogy of the seminar is inherent in its design — the teacher is a coach, a guide, a navigator of a student-centered discussion. The curriculum, so often driven by content which "must" be covered, is now transformed into the agent which will best *serve* the *outcome* which is valued! Once again, the simple process of *planning backwards from outcomes* informs curriculum design and instructional practice in a manner which is natural and organic — not contrived to suit the ends of content coverage.

What Socratic Seminars can do, then, is genuinely liberate teachers from the oppression and pressures of content coverage. Is there a district in this country which does not claim to value *effective listening* as an outcome? How many goals or objectives statements present *effective communication in writing **and speaking*** as an end? If those outcomes are stated, how are they being achieved? Are those goals *only* the domain of Language Arts, Social Studies, and various Humanities teachers? Do Science, Math, Technology, Physical Education, and so on, have **no responsibility** to insure that students graduate with the important outcomes we claim we want them to have? Where *is* the accountability?

The fact of the matter is, Socratic Seminars allow teachers in *all* disciplines to meet the goals of "effective speaking and listening" along with a host of other higher-order thinking skills outcomes. Which brings us back to the selection of a "text." Because the focus of the seminar is intensive, texts chosen are often short selections or excerpts from longer works — whether it's from a novel, a film, part of a musical score, a section of a painting, one phase of an experiment, a single line from a mathematic theorem. Again, this should prove liberating to the teacher. From the vast array of material available within or across disciplines, teachers can choose that text which is most appropriate in promoting student learning — with depth and perseverance. As is noted later, teachers, no matter what their discipline area, use a vast array of sources in seminar — and many use the same text, even though they teach different subjects!

Once the outcomes are clear and the text is decided upon, the teacher or teachers must then develop an opening question. The importance of this opening question cannot be understated. In *Introducing the Socratic Seminar into the Secondary Classroom* (1991), produced by the Chicago Board of Education, the opening pages are quite clear: "The Socratic Seminar begins with an opening question for which there is no single expected response. A good opening question should generate the conversation for the duration of the seminar" (p. 3). Dennis Gray's advice for opening questions is as follows:

- They arise from genuine curiosity on the part of the leader.
- They have no single or "right" answer.
- They are framed to generate dialogue leading to greater understanding of the ideas in the text.
- They can best be answered by reference to the text.

(Adapted from a worksheet handout, 1993)

This is not as easy to create as it may seem, and collaboration between teachers in developing opening questions is often helpful. The teacher/Seminar leader should probably have several questions prepared — all of which follow Gray's basic guidelines — to insure engagement which engenders deep thinking. Chicago's *Introducing* resource book suggests "opening question strategies" which ask students to examine the text carefully and "relate (it) to their immediate environment," or to focus on "key words and phrases" or, "prepare a question and bring it to the seminar" (all quotes from p. 20). The significant aspect of the opening question is that it is designed as a launch pad *for the students*. While the teacher is a member of the discussion and initially its leader, the text and the meaning *the students* make of the text are what Socratic Seminars are about. They become a wonderful vehicle for students to clearly demonstrate what they know and are able to do in a very public arena — and are, therefore, extremely powerful performance assessments.

A VARIETY OF IMPLEMENTATIONS

Just as the Seminar can be used to meet any number of outcomes, Seminars, themselves, can be implemented in any number of ways. In some schools they are used as part of a Graduation Exhibition; in others, as a classroom assessment device; in still others, as an "exit" exhibition to move on to the next level of schooling. Whether they are part of a Humanities team assessment or an interdisciplinary activity, Socratic Seminars, and their attendant exercises, are powerful feedback devices for gauging student skills and progress. As important, they provide students with an excellent, active vehicle for self-assessment. Particularly through the use of videotaped Seminars, students can assess their own performance, make note of what's strong and what "needs work," and set realistic goals for improvement — all in the context of clearly identified outcomes of significance. Seminars, then, not only clarify the curriculum, instruction, and assessment relationship for students and teachers, but also serve as beacons for the progress of student work and the school's curricular program. It can help answer a question *everyone* in a school should be asking: *Am I making progress toward the goals I think are most important?*

It seems only appropriate that much early work in Socratic Seminars occurred in Adler's home base, Chicago. The citywide resource book for introducing Seminars was made available in 1991, prompted, to a great extent by the use of the Socratic method at Sullivan High School. As described by Eileen Barton in *Graduation by Exhibition: Assessing Genuine Achievement* (ASCD, 1993), Sullivan High School instituted "Diploma by Exhibition" in the spring of 1989. Their system grew out of a desire to exhibit what students knew and were able to do in ways traditional testing could not. Sullivan's senior class that year had already engaged in Socratic Seminars, so this was not new to them — but the stakes were certainly raised! The faculty at Sullivan also decided students would have to write a composition in conjunction with their Seminar experience to receive credit for graduation.

The initial Graduation Exhibition Seminars would use four texts (*Why War?* by Freud, *The Gettysburg Address*, and two short stories about the Civil War by Ambrose Bierce) and students would have to write a follow-up essay chosen from several topics presented *after* their Seminar discussion concluded. Rather than restate what is already well-documented by Barton, let's focus on those aspects of the Seminar and its follow-up writing assignment which speak to the issues related to assessment.

> As seminars got underway throughout the building, students and teachers found themselves caught up in the intensity of the discussions. Students showed obvious preparation and thought. Anxious teachers felt their concerns about mixed academic levels melt away as students listened to one another, shared ideas, and worked together to reach an understanding of the readings. After 90 minutes, the bell ending the seminar caught many students and teachers by surprise. . . .
> (Teachers) were impressed by the seriousness and maturity with which students approached the seminar, and the students ability to sustain an extended discussion of the readings.
>
> *Graduation by Exhibition*, p. 37

What Barton goes on to point out is that the written follow-up essays "contrasted markedly with the sophistication of the seminars" (p. 38). In fact, 40% of the students had to rewrite their compositions to attain the level acceptable for graduation. The importance of this revelation is noted by Barton:

> Having undertaken the Diploma by Exhibition as a means of assessing the the effectiveness of our educational program, we concluded that we had to pay serious attention to the teaching of writing.
>
> *Graduation by Exhibition*, p. 39

Consider, then, what Sullivan High School learned about its students and its academic program by implementing Socratic Seminars as a high-stakes assessment instrument. Not only were students' strengths and weaknesses presented to the faculty, but the effectiveness of the faculty's work with those students was subject to scrutiny, too. Eileen Barton also points out that teachers from across all the discipline areas served as seminar leaders — having first participated in faculty seminars on the readings.

The monograph goes on to describe the second and third years of implementation, but the significant point to note is the powerful affect the seminar had on the students *and* teachers. Math teachers would now lead seminars on Abbott's *Flatlands* or Euclid's *Elements*, as a means of preparing students for their final exhibition. But this also allowed those teachers to see their students in a different light, as problemsolvers and thinkers in a different context. And, it gives a teacher feedback as to how effectively she or he is presenting concepts and ideas, as well as mechanical procedures. In all, the Socratic Seminar is a valuable assessment tool to have in one's repertoire and Sullivan High School pioneered its use in a compelling and powerful way.

ATTAINING MIDDLE SCHOOL EXIT OUTCOMES

The Academy for the Middle Years–NorthWest (AMY–NW) in Philadelphia, has used Socratic Seminars as part of their curriculum, instruction, and assessment system for a number of years, with most of the staff trained as Seminar Leaders. In their experience, a number of variations on the Seminar process have emerged, pointing to the flexibility of this assessment to serve the needs of its learning community. A fine example of this is Gert Kline's 1993–94 school year 8th grade mathematics class.

A 90-minute block alternate day schedule (classes meet for 90 minutes every other day, rather than 45 minutes every day) created an interesting possibility for the math teacher. Each week one or two of her classes would have *three* 90-minute blocks to meet. Gert Kline and the school librarian, Janet Malloy, decided to use that third meeting for Socratic Seminars. Part of the motivation, Kline says, was to get students to "think 'differently' than they were used to when in Math class" (personal correspondence). By having two teachers in the room at once, one could lead the Seminar while the other made observations, and sometimes participated — a technique other teams of teachers often use with Seminars. But Kline and Malloy devised some other protocols for their 8th graders which are not only developmentally appropriate, but speak to the concept of teachers-as-curriculum and assessment-designers.

One of their first decisions was that assignments were not given prior to seminar. Rather, readings, tapes, or artwork which could be "digested" in 15–20 minutes were used. Sometimes selections were read together aloud, other times in groups, and still other times silently as individuals. In some cases, during the opening segment a "preseminar" minilesson was used to examine concepts like sequencing or analogies. After this activity, students would be given the opening question and the Seminar would begin.

Because of the age of the participants, certain other procedures were created. While students might be permitted to sit where they wanted, there were times when designated seating was used to spread out the more vocal students. Another technique developed was to appoint three "observers" who would monitor the discussion, specifically observing one set of students. This was another way to remove those most vocal students (giving quieter students greater opportunity to participate) while still engaging them in a useful and important role. The teachers also made sure there was always time to conduct a "postseminar" activity, usually a writing exercise, so students would reflect on the Seminar discussion and commit their thoughts to writing.

A variety of forms were created for students and teachers to use to not only evaluate the Seminar, but to also consider what had been learned during the discussion. Several of these forms are presented in the following pages, with commentary as to how they help make the Seminar a more effective assessment tool. What these forms, as well as the topics discussed in Seminar, illustrate, is that when teachers focus on important outcomes, they may move "outside" their discipline area. In this case, Gert Kline, a math teacher, focused on outcomes like *asking questions* and *listening to answers*, the discussion skills of *speaking* and *responding*, as well as *collaboration*. So, while not directly linked to mathematics outcomes, the Seminars were part of the larger goals connected to 8th grade exit outcomes at AMY–NW, which *every* teacher has responsibility for.

A common, early Seminar topic which many teachers use is "The Pledge of Allegiance." AMY–NW is no exception, but their procedure is an interesting one and worth examining. As a preseminar activity students are asked to write the Pledge as they know it. The opening question was: "If you could, would you change the Pledge of Allegiance?" Students voted using "yes/no" cards to indicate their response and the discussion then revolved around defending their decision. As a postseminar activity, students were asked to rewrite the Pledge as they believed it should read. Simple in design, this is a wonderful assessment which requires students to not only engage in higher-order thinking (analysis, evaluation), but also taps into numerous exit outcome skills related to reading, writing, speaking, and listening!

In another Seminar period, students examined the Horace Pippin painting "Mr. Prejudice." The worksheet the teachers used for this seminar is included below (Fig. 4.1), to show how teachers (particularly those working in teams) can organize and execute an effective seminar. The students were not given the title to the painting, and that fact created the opening question: *What would be a good title for this painting?* In reviewing the teachers' "Mr. Prejudice" organizing/planning sheet, note that prompts for the students were on the blackboard *before* the students were even given copies of the painting. As with any effective teaching strategy — but particularly in the case of an effective *assessment* strategy — careful planning done beforehand will ensure greater results for the students. In this case, the use of prompts as part of the preseminar activity, the "round robin" eliciting of student responses, and the listing of those responses on chart paper, along with the brief biography of Horace Pippin, serve as excellent preparation for the Seminar discussion period. Asking students to respond in writing as to the appropriateness of the title — and then *sharing* those responses — is an equally effective postseminar activity. Again, these are 8th graders who need a structure in their routine, but are also, as Gert Kline notes, "interested in talking and expressing opinions." What they learn in a Seminar, according to Kline, is "the skill of referencing statements to fact (text) and . . . of defending or supporting a statement or opinion."

The following pages present the "Mr. Prejudice" planning form from the teachers (Fig. 4.1); a "Listening and Speaking in Seminar" sheet (Fig. 4.2) which not only focuses students on the goals of the discussion but provides prompts for thinking about the Seminar; the Observation Form (Fig. 4.3) student observers use; and the Facilitator's Evaluation Sheet (Fig. 4.4). Each of these forms reveals important aspects of the Socratic Seminar as an assessment instrument.

The "Listening and Speaking" form enunciates outcomes; the student observers sheet requires careful attention to detail in speaking and listening, being able to identify paraphrasing, and so on. The Facilitators sheet is clearly aimed at critical self-reflection by the teachers, examining the effectiveness of their Seminar.

From Gert Kline's point of view, the value of Socratic Seminar is broad. Beyond the skills and other outcomes it can address, there are certain intangibles rubrics might never reveal. Some of her reflections on Seminar are revealing, indeed.

> As their Math teacher, I saw some students in a very different light. Students who were uncomfortable in Math class were very vocal in seminar; conversely, students who were "big talkers" when it came to "he said, she said" business, had very little to say when they were required to support an opinion. Students who did not participate vocally turned out to be good writers. When we discovered this, Janet and I made it a point of having everyone read their writing at the end of seminar. This way all were guaranteed a voice.
>
> I think the other benefit to the students that emerged from seminar was that during "family group" discussions (advisories), even though the rules (of seminar) were not imposed, they acted as though they existed. The result was that, for the most part, the discussions were decent, respectful, and usually fruitful!

The benefit these kinds of observations can add to a teacher's knowledge of his or her students is invaluable — and is not the kind of information traditional testing can provide us about learning styles, student thinking, and so on.

Reviewing Gert Kline's remarks about seminar, and examining the way she and Janet Malloy implemented the discussions — carefully considering the student population they were serving — the value of Socratic Seminars as an additional assessment in a teacher's

(Text continues on page 106.)

**FIGURE 4.1: ACADEMY FOR THE MIDDLE YEARS, NORTHWEST —
"MR. PREJUDICE"**

"MR. PREJUDICE" by Horace Pippin
Wednesday, April 27, 1994

[ON BOARD: "I see...," "I observe...," "I notice...]

9:00 - 9:30 PRE-SEMINAR (Gert; Janet, recording)

-Point out phrases on the board and explain how they are to be used.
-Distribute copies of painting.
-2-3 minutes for silent observations; suggest that students may want
 to list observations.
-"Round robin" observing using phrases on board.
-List observations on chart paper.

9:30 - 9:40 Biography of Horace Pippin (Janet)

9:40 - 10:10 SEMINAR (Gert)

Opening Question: **WHAT WOULD BE A GOOD TITLE FOR THIS
PAINTING?**

10:10 - 10:20 POST-SEMINAR (Janet)

-Give actual title.
     -Distribute paper.
     -Write opinion: IS THIS TITLE APPROPRIATE? SUPPORT YOUR
          ANSWER.

10:20 - 10:30 SHARING OF WRITTEN RESPONSES (Gert & Janet)

FIGURE 4.2: ACADEMY FOR THE MIDDLE YEARS, NORTHWEST — LISTENING AND SPEAKING IN SEMINAR

One goal of seminars is to understand the ideas and thoughts of others through asking questions and listening to answers.   This means that seminar participants must practice how to agree and how to disagree.

Use the ways of responding listed below before you speak. Remember, we're building on ways to speak, respond in seminar and participate in discussions in a calm and collaborative manner.

1. I agree with _____ because, but I want to add another reason why I think _____ is true.
   (Give another reason) _____

   _____

   _____

   _____

2. I disagree with _____ because _____

   _____

   _____

   _____

3. I'm not sure why _____ said _____.   Can you repeat that in another way so I can understand?

4. I can see your point, _____, but I want to add/disagree/give another side: _____

   _____

   _____

   _____

5. This is what I think you are saying?   Is that right?

   _____

   _____

This page intentionally blank.

FIGURE 4.3: ACADEMY FOR THE MIDDLE YEARS, NORTHWEST— SOCRATIC SEMINAR OBSERVATION FORM

OBSERVER _____   DATE _____   ADVISORY _____

READING/ITEM _____

OPENING QUESTION _____

Persons Observed	Uses Text	Listens +/o	Responds to Q =	Paraphrases	Asks Q	Defers	Comments -- use numbers or words
1.							
2.							
3.							
4.							
5.							
6.							

*Comments -- use these numbers for comments:

1. needs to speak more
2. playful
3. calls out; interrupts
4. plays with namecard or other things
5. needs to listen more carefully, asks for repeated comments

6. has an excellent idea
7. asks a good question
8. outstanding participation includes responding, asking questions paraphrasing, and deferring

What is the best idea you heard in seminar?

How would you rate the seminar? (check one)

_____ Excellent (Everyone listened, participated, had good ideas, did not interrupt)

_____ Good (Generally, everyone participated but the seminar could have better ideas and behavior)

_____ Fair (Side talk, interruptions, students distracted)

_____ Poor (Lots of side talk, interruptions, rude behavior)

How many times did the facilitator have to stop seminar? _____

FIGURE 4.4: ACADEMY FOR THE MIDDLE YEARS, NORTHWEST — FACILITATOR'S EVALUATION SHEET

DATE _____   NAME _____
                          GROUP _____

FACILITATOR'S EVALUATION SHEET

READING/ITEM _____

_____

                                                    <u>YES</u>   <u>NO</u>   <u>N/A</u>

1. Were the participants engaged early?

2. Did you make sure the questions were understood?

3. Did you ask questions which led to further questions?

4. Did you use answers as the basis of follow-up questions?

5. Did you allow for discussion of disagreement?

6. Did you listen carefully to participants' statements?

7. Did you accept participants' answers without judgment?

8. Did you keep attention on ideas in text/item being discussed?

9. Did you behave as a good model of seminar participation?

10. Did you correct misreadings of the text?

11. Did you allow time (pauses) for thinking?

12. Did you draw out reasons and implication?

13. Did you or did you not reach closure?

DATE _____   NAME _____
                       GROUP _____

FACILITATOR'S EVALUATION SHEET

IN THE COURSE OF THE SEMINAR:

What was the most interesting question? _____

_____

What was the most interesting idea to come from a participant? _____

_____

What was the best thing you observed? _____

_____

What was the most troubling thing you observed? _____

_____

What did you think should be done differently in the next seminar? _____

_____

repertoire becomes apparent. As Kline commented: "I really enjoyed the freedom to teach by theme, project, or unit as long as I was *providing the necessary skills required for exiting 8th Grade*" (emphasis added). Not only are students provided with an instructional mode which teaches or reinforces necessary and important skills, but teachers are allowed to push their own pedagogy into new areas, learning more about their students and themselves. Adapting the basic concept to fit the students — academically, developmentally, etc. — the Socratic Seminar broadens the horizon of the classroom, the students, and the teachers.

SEMINARS AS UNIT ASSESSMENTS

Fulton Valley Prep at Piner High School is in Santa Rosa, California, and is a member of The Coalition of Essential Schools. Its implementation of Socratic Seminars adds another dimension to our view of how Seminars can operate.

Starting with the format of "Where are we going?," "How will we get there?," and "How will we know if we've arrived?," the Spring 1994, Humanities course examined America in the 1920s and 1930s (Fig. 4.5). Driven by the essential question, *What should high school graduates know about the 1920s and 1930s?*, students were expected to read at least one novel which would be discussed in a Seminar format. Looking at the assignment sheet ("Boom to Bust Exhibition #1: Literature Seminar") (Fig. 4.6), we can see how the Piner teachers adapted the Seminar to the student population and their outcomes. As with earlier assessments, rubrics are provided for students *before* the assessment task begins! And, following the common practice suggested by Adler in 1982, a follow-up writing assignment is required (Fig. 4.7).

Let's review the Piner Seminar assignment considering the following:

- What are the desired outcomes (skills/content/dispositions)?

- What are the expectations for the students? (If you were a student, what would you think is expected of you?)

- How are students guided to, and through, their Seminar?

♦ How do the rubrics help define or clarify the desired
outcomes?

It's important to note, again, that the Seminar and its follow-up
essay were only one part of three requirements for this unit. With
that in mind, what information about student achievement and
progress might the Seminar reveal which the other assessments
would not?

Content and skills outcomes are defined for the Fulton Valley
Prep students several ways: the "Where are we going?" and "How
will we get there?" introductory piece (Fig. 4.5); the "Literature
Seminar" assignment sheet (Fig. 4.6); and the Seminar and Essay
rubrics (Fig. 4.7). Initially, we can see that the assignment is going
to ask students to think critically about *what* facts (about the '20s
and '30s) are important to know — and why. Next, students are
informed that they will "research, talk, listen, and think about the
history of the Jazz Age and the Depression." Clearly, reading,
writing, speaking, and listening skills are goals which are embedded
in the content of the history and literature of the period.

Disposition or attitude outcomes are found — implicitly and
explicitly — in the "Literature Seminar" assignment sheet (Fig. 4.6).
Choosing a text, acting responsibly (bring it to class, read during
time provided), contributing to group discussions, maintaining
a journal, meeting deadlines, are all work habits, dispositions, and
attitudes, which are promoted throughout the assignment. The
expectations for the students are clear — here is what you need
to do to be successful in this task. The introductory paragraphs and
the nine steps presented to students on the "Literature Seminar"
assignment sheet are not purely informational. They are designed
to reinforce and promote those habits which are valued, and they
are a statement of expectations for students to live up to. Most
important — they are *clear.* Reading this assignment, it is hard to
imagine that students would not have a clear idea of what the
expectations *and the process necessary to achieve those expectations* are.

If the assignment sheet was not clear enough, however, students
also have the Seminar and Essay Rubrics (Fig. 4.7) to refer to.

(Text continues on page 112.)

FIGURE 4.5: PINER HIGH SCHOOL — HUMANITIES CURRICULUM

Fulton Valley Prep at Piner High School
Humanities Curriculum
Third quarter, Spring 1994

Where are we going?
When your parents (and your FVP teachers) went to high school, the study of U.S. History usually meant listening to lectures, reading textbooks and answering the questions at the end of the chapter, memorizing tons of facts for the test (multiple choice and short answer) and, for many students, promptly forgetting most of those facts right after the test.

Today in Fulton Valley Prep, we believe that facts are less important than understanding, that teachers can't pour information into students' heads like milk into a glass and that true learning must be active.

But what about all those facts? Shouldn't we all know some of them? Which ones? Is there any information that is crucial for all Americans to know?

Our fourth area of focus this year in Humanities will be on Boom to Bust: from the Jazz Age to the Depression years. As we learn about this turbulent era, we will grapple with the following essential question: **What should high school graduates know about the 1920's and 1930's?**

How will we get there?
As we explore the essential question, we will immerse ourselves in the events, the personalities, the beliefs, the music, literature and art of the period between the two World Wars. We will see documentaries and feature films about the 20's and 30's. We will listen to jazz and blues and swing. We will read novels and poetry and essays from the era. We will look at photographs and paintings. We will invest in (well, okay... only with play money) and learn about the stock market . We will research, talk, listen and think about the history of the Jazz Age and the Depression years.

How will we know if we've arrived?
Students will exhibit knowledge and skills gained during the unit by:
  (1) participating in a *Socratic Seminar* and writing a follow-up essay on one of several novels set in the 20's or 30's;
  (2) reporting on results of five or six weeks of "investing" in the stock market; and
  (3) creating learning materials (HyperCard/ text/ multimedia) which will enable other high school students to learn what you have decided is essential about the period.

FIGURE 4.6: PINER HIGH SCHOOL —
ASSIGNMENT SHEET: LITERATURE SEMINAR

Boom to Bust Exhibition #1: Literature Seminar

What should high school graduates know about the 1920s and 1930s?

One of the most enjoyable ways to learn about our past is through literature. Poems, stories, and novels written during and about these times reveal insights into the lives of people who lived through these turbulent decades. What was it like to be a flapper during the Roaring Twenties? What happened to families as they struggled through the financial hardships of the Depression years? Pieces of the puzzle that make up our American past will fit into place as we read.

For this exhibition you will read at least one novel (from a list of four or five choices) that was written during or about the 20s or 30s. The public "exhibition" of what you learned from your reading will take place in a Socratic Seminar with other students who have read the same book. The purpose of the Socratic Seminar is to examine the text closely and thoughtfully in order to enlarge our understanding of the book itself and the times it was written to portray. After *active* participation in the seminar, you will write an essay defending your position on a central question about the book.

1. Choose one or two books from the list that most interest you.

2. Bring your book to class daily, and read during the time provided.

3. Use your letter journal to record your ideas and questions, and communicate them to your teacher and classmates.

4. Participate in practice seminars on poems and short stories of the times in order to gain confidence and master the skills of discussing a text in this format.

5. Complete all class activities designed to help you better understand the book you have chosen to read.

6. Read the entire text and mark important passages with Post-It Notes before your scheduled seminar date.

7. *Participate actively in the formal Socratic Seminar scheduled for the book that you have read. Ask questions, state opinions, and *back up your ideas with evidence from your reading.*

8. Formulate a thesis based on your response to the opening Seminar question and the discussion of the text(s) that follows.reading of the book, and the discussion during Seminar.

9. *Write an essay exploring your thesis.

 *Both the seminar and the essay are required for credit.

FIGURE 4.7: PINER HIGH SCHOOL—
LITERATURE SEMINAR AND ESSAY RUBRIC

Boom to Bust Exhibition #1: Literature Seminar and Essay Rubric

SEMINAR (credit/no credit)

Oral Participation	1. Addresses the question using evidence from the book. Cites examples, passages, characters from the book to support answers. Comments show that student has read and understood the book and is making connections between the book and the ideas generated by the seminar.
	2. Makes relevant comments during the seminar which show response to previous speakers' ideas. Helps to enlarge understanding of the text and ideas generated in the seminar.
	3. Takes the initiative in participating; does not have to be prompted.
	4. May ask questions to clarify and deepen the discussion of ideas.
Other Participation	1. Is on time for the seminar.
	2. Shows attentiveness through body language: sitting up straight, looking at the speaker, giving the speaker the floor.
	3. Does not belittle or criticize others' comments.

ESSAY

	Mastery	Distinguished
Content	1. The essay has a thesis which answers the seminar's opening question.	1. The essay has a clear thesis which answers the seminar's opening question. The thesis refers specifically to the book.
	2. The thesis is supported by ideas which show an understanding of the book.	2. The thesis is supported by connected ideas which show a depth of understanding of the ideas from the book. There is creative and original thinking.
	3. The essay refers to the book to back up ideas. The author's name is cited.	3. The writer cites evidence from the book using examples, quotes, and/or passages to support ideas. The writer uses the author's name effectively.
	4. The writer clearly understands the book's storyline and can apply one idea from the book to	4. It is clear from the writer's discussion of ideas that he/she has read and understood the novel in depth and can apply its ideas to other situations.
Format / Mechanics	1. The essay is organized so that each paragraph contains one idea. There are some transitions to connect ideas and/or paragraphs.	1. The essay is well-organized, logically presented, with transitions to connect ideas and sections.
	2. The opening paragraph is to the point. The closing paragraph concludes the essay by briefly summarizing main points and restating the thesis.	2. The essay contains an interesting opening and a solid conclusion. The conclusion avoids repetition yet restates the thesis and main ideas.
	3. Same as distinguished, but hand-written in ink, single-spaced.	3. Quotation marks are used to identify short quotes; quotes longer than one line are set off separately. Book titles are underlined, paragraphs are indented, and the essay is typed and double-spaced, with no errors.

Returning to the Content and Skills domains, these rubrics also clarify the expectations for students. By dividing the "oral participation" and "other participation" into two categories for the Seminar, the Humanities team has made a significant distinction for the students to take note of. The "oral participation" indicators in the rubric clearly illustrate the active role which is expected of students during the Seminar. "Other participation" focuses on punctuality and respect — valued outcomes, too, but distinct from the active, oral participation described in the first half of the rubric.

The Essay Rubric also clarifies expectations and outcomes for students by presenting a grid which distinguishes between the "Content" of student writing and the "Mechanics" of it. Too often rubrics for writing focus on the simple mechanical aspects of the task (correct paragraphing, spelling, punctuation, etc.) and fail to investigate the *quality* of the content of student writing. As mentioned earlier, these rubrics are not perfect, **but** they certainly help guide students to the outcomes of significance. By creating the categories of "Mastery" and "Distinguished" the Humanities Team has "notified" students that they are, indeed, pushing for a high-quality product.

How does the Socratic Seminar portion of this assessment broaden teachers' understanding of student progress and achievement? By requiring students to participate in Seminar, and producing a rubric which clearly rewards *active* student involvement, teachers can discover which students can articulate their ideas about their reading. Which students have read deeply and analytically? Who seems to know the basics of the book but has trouble articulating those ideas — and what do we need to do to help that student improve his or her performance? Which students have clearly marked their texts and can quickly refer to passages of significance, and who is struggling with what skill (reading comprehension; taking notes while reading)? Who is developing the ability to ask probing questions? Who reinforces comments by classmates and builds on their ideas?

Few of these skills can be measured by traditional tests — or by simply reading student essays. As pointed out in the earlier example of Sullivan High School, students may express themselves very well in Seminar, but have problems with their writing. And, as the AMY–NW example shows, some who are quiet may be quite adept with their writing and need to learn to vocalize their thoughts publicly. This is where the Socratic Seminar is so useful as an assessment tool. Because it *focuses* student work on a particular text and demands an intensive examination of that text. And, because it asks for students to present their ideas in a discussion format, the Socratic Seminar creates a setting where teachers can *observe* their students' thinking! Since the teacher is a coach, guide, facilitator, and *not* the center of attention through which all information must flow, there is time to "step back" and assess the progress students are making in their discussion, public speaking, and listening skills. If these are, in fact, outcomes which we believe are important for students to graduate with, then the Socratic Seminar becomes an integral part of the assessment system.

What we can learn from the Piner example is how an assessment *system* can be developed which addresses the learning styles and multiple intelligences of our students. By incorporating the Socratic Seminar method in an exhibition context which has several other assessment components, as Piner has, the Humanities team is creating a system which provides students and teachers with valuable feedback about student achievement and progress in a variety of contexts. It demystifies the assessment process, makes the outcomes and expectations clear, and provides one more window into the realm of student thinking and learning, improving the teaching/learning context for everyone concerned.

STARTING OVER:
INTRODUCING SOCRATIC SEMINARS TO NOVICES

Working at North Shore High School in Glen Head, New York, Carlo Rebolini was teamed with Eric Sundberg in a Humanities team which used Socratic Seminars as an integral part of their assessment system. Sundberg's rubric for Seminars has been popularized by both Grant Wiggins and Dennis Gray (an adaptation is presented later in this chapter in the Bronxville High School example) and is a fine example of how important habits for student learning and outcomes can be presented. When Rebolini moved to Garden City High School on Long Island for the 1994–95 school year, he introduced the Seminar method in his 9th grade English classes. The example presented below illustrates how a teacher can begin to develop a culture for thoughtful discussion to students.

Faced with a student population unaccustomed to the rigorous discussion skills the Socratic Seminar requires, Rebolini was essentially starting from scratch. Because of this, he wisely introduced the Seminar process incrementally, melding it in units which still called for traditional assessment measures, but "upping the ante" for students by building in a discussion component as part of their grades. By including outcomes which can only be attained through the Socratic Seminar method — developing a vocabulary for articulating close reading and critical thinking skills, for example — Rebolini started with a short story unit.

Initially, guiding the students through two short stories (Lawrence's "The Rocking-Horse Winner" and Achebe's "Marriage is a Private Affair"), an examination of story elements such as plot, theme, character, setting, and tone were discussed traditionally. Building on that method, though, Rebolini required his students to break into small groups to concentrate on one of the stories, and gave each group the responsibility of leading the class in a discussion about one of those aspects of the story. In this way, students were asked to begin probing deeper into the stories, not settling for the simple superficial elements of story analysis. Students would also have to complete a writing assignment connected to their story.

With that groundwork done, Rebolini then introduced students to the Socratic Seminar method, clearly delineating how this kind of discussion is different from what had gone on so far. Explaining that they would participate in a Socratic Seminar using a story they *had not yet seen*, the teacher also walked through the rubric with the students, answering questions, clarifying, and explaining how the rubric helps define the Seminar itself. The text for the Seminar would be Chekov's short story "The Bet," which the students would have 2 days to prepare.

What were the teachers goals in this initial foray? As described by Rebolini:

> I was looking for some evidence that students were able to critically analyze the story using, where appropriate, some of the terms we had discussed. Additionally, I was looking for intelligent insights supported by textual references. Class participation in traditional discussions had been disappoint-

ing, and I was hoping that the Socratic Seminar format would increase participation.

Aside from using the rubric to evaluate student performance, Carlo developed a checksheet for his students with a simple key. Using a class roster list, he monitored student participation by putting a checkmark next to a student's name when a comment was made, a "Q" for a question, a "T" for a textual reference, a "P" for a paraphrase, and a "D" for "directly called upon" (for a response). A quick scan of this list quickly identified those students who participated most and least, how much questioning went on, who was able to paraphrase, and so on. What is significant about this innovation is that it formalizes a way many teachers informally assess their students now. It also points to the value of the Socratic Seminar method. Because the students are conducting the discussion, the teacher can, in fact, monitor what is going on in a more formal fashion, documenting the actual interchanges. Rebolini even included an area for additional anecdotal comments at the bottom of his roster, so as to note particular performances.

This formal operationalizing of discussion assessment is important to note. As mentioned at the opening of the chapter, "class discussion" and "class participation" are often used to reward or punish students by bumping grades up or down at report card time. Too often, the reference point for student participation and discussion is the teacher's memory and little else. By instituting Seminars in which students carry the responsibility for the progress of the discussion, the teacher is freed to more formally document and assess what students are **actually** doing — a vast improvement over what presently exists.

Returning to Rebolini's classroom and his novice 9th graders discussion of Chekov's "The Bet," the description of "what happened" is revealing.

> I began the seminar with the question, "Who won the bet and why?" What ensued was, by far, the liveliest discussion the class had participated in since the beginning of the school year. Students were animated in their responses. They referred to the text where appropriate. Clearly, they were analyzing the text, thinking aloud, and basing their insights on what had obviously been a close reading of the

text. Their texts were well annotated with definitions, questions, and comments. What did not happen was the incorporation of some of the terms we had defined in their in their comments. In their debriefing, students raved about the seminar experience. They agreed that they left with a better understanding of the text, and they sought to gain assurance from me that more seminars would follow. That, of course, was given.

The fact that Carlo Rebolini is an experienced Seminar leader no doubt contributed greatly to the success of this initial Socratic experience for his students. As significant, though, is the *process* he used in planning and executing this work with his novice 9th graders — an important lesson regarding the implementation of any performance assessment.

By developing Socratic Seminars organically, as a natural outgrowth of class discussion to group-led discussion to Seminar discussion, the students were given time to learn how to take some responsibility for class conversation. Also, presenting students with an explanation of what the Seminar is (presented in the following pages as Fig. 4.8) and sharing the rubric for evaluation with them, they had the opportunity to ask questions, clarify points, and not feel that this new method was sprung on them. Because the new assessment was presented in stages, with clear explanations every step of the way, the students were much more invested in it — they knew what was going on, what was going to be expected, and how they were going to be assessed.

As with other performance assessments, Socratic Seminars are an effective tool for teachers to use in evaluating their own work. How effectively are we teaching students? What can *see* in their performance which we can attribute to our curriculum/instruction/assessment design? When asked what *he* learned from this experience, Carlo Rebolini said this:

(Text continues on page 120.)

FIGURE 4.8: GARDEN CITY HIGH SCHOOL —
ASSESSMENT CRITERIA FOR SOCRATIC SEMINARS

English Department   Mr. Rebolini
Socratic Seminars

One skill that we are seeking to develop this year is the ability to express an analysis of a text both in writing and speaking. The analysis should be reasonable and supported with textual evidence. The expression of that analysis should be concisely and clearly presented.

One way to develop that skills in speaking is through student participation in Socratic seminars. A Socratic seminar is a discussion focusing on a single text. The discussion is initiated by a question posed by the teacher. What follows is a lively analysis of the text where students develop an interpretation based and built on what other students are saying. Students pose questions of one another. The rules of the regular class are suspended. Student do not have to raise their hands, and they sit in a circle.

The final part of a Socratic seminar is a brief assessment of the success of the seminar. During this period, call debriefing, students evaluate their own performances and the effectiveness of the seminar itself. The primary question addressed is do students leave with a better, richer understanding of the text than that they came in with.

Student performance during the seminar is graded based on four criteria: listening, conduct, thinking/reasoning and reading. A scoring guide outlining in these criteria will be discussed.

Excellent:

A. Conduct: Demonstrates clear respect for the learning process and patience with different opinions and complexity. Shows initiative by asking others for clarification, bringing others into the conversation, and moving the conversation forward. Speaks to all participants (not just the teacher or a single student). Avoids talking too much, too long, too softly. Avoids nit-picking and inappropriate language.

B. Speaking/Reasoning: Understands questions before answering. Cites evidence from the text (or elsewhere when appropriate). Expresses complete thoughts in complete sentences. Comments are logical and insightful and move the conversation forward. Makes connections among ideas from previous speakers or resolves seemingly contradictory ideas. Considers all sources, not just his or her own. Avoids bad logic.

C. Listening: Pays attention to details, writes down questions and thoughts. Responses take into account the comments of other participants and demonstrates that the student has kept up. Points out bad logic. Overcomes distractions.

D. Reading: Student is thoroughly familiar with the text and has come prepared with notes and question in the margins. Key words, phrases, and ideas are underlines and possible contradiction have been identified. Pronounces words perfectly.

Good:

A. Conduct: Generally shows composure but may display some impatience with contrary or confusing ideas. Comments often enough but does not necessarily encourage others to participate. May tend to address only the teacher or get into debates.

B. Speaking/Reasoning: Responds to question voluntarily. Comments indicate student has given thought to the text but may not show appreciation of subtler points within it. Comments are logical but may not make connections among ideas of previous speakers. Ideas are interesting enough that other participants respond to them.

C. Listening: Generally pays attention and responds thoughtfully to ideas and questions of other participants and the teacher. Absorption in one's own idea my distract the student from some other participants' ideas.

D. Reading: Has read the text and comes with some questions and ideas regarding it. These may not all be written out in advance. While student has a good understanding of the vocabulary, he may mispronounce some new or foreign words.

Fair:

A. Conduct: Student participate and expresses a belief that his ideas are important in understanding the text. May sometimes lose composure and interfere with the learning process. Having at least read the text the participant may make some insightful comments, however, insisting too forcefully, or by not participating enough, the participant may not contribute much to the progress of the conversation. Tends to debate rather than discuss or shows understanding but only when called upon.

B. Speaking/Reasoning: Responds to questions but may have to be called upon. Comments indicate that the student has read the text but has not put much effort in preparing questions and ideas for the seminar. Comments may not take into account some important details and may not always flow logically from the conversation. While not being quite wrong, ideas may not flow logically from previous comments or questions.

C. Listening: Appears to find some ideas unimportant while responding to others. May need to have some questions repeated while not asking to have confusing questions restated. Takes few notes during the seminar.

D. Reading: Appears to have read or skimmed the text, but the text is not marked with meaningful notes or questions. May show difficulty with some vocabulary and mispronounce important words. Key concepts may be misunderstood. There is little evidence of serious reflection done prior to the seminar.

Unsatisfactory:

A. Conduct: Displays little respect for the learning process. If participating at all the student may be argumentative. Minor distractions are taken advantage of. May use inappropriate language and speak about individuals rather than ideas. Arrives unprepared without notes, a pencil, perhaps event the text.

B. Speaking/Reasoning: Extremely reluctant to participate, even when called upon. Comments are so illogical as to be meaningless. May mumble or express incomplete ideas. Little or no account is made of previous comments or important ideas in the text.

C. Listening: Appears uninvolved in the seminar. Comments may display complete misinterpretations of questions or comments of other participants.

D. Reading: Student is clearly unprepared for seminar. Important words. phrases, or ideas in the text are unfamiliar. There are not notes or questions marked on the text and no attempt has been made to get help with difficult reading.

First, the experience reaffirmed for me what I had already known — namely, that Socratic Seminar is a powerful teaching tool which allows students to formulate an analysis of a text independent of teacher direction. The experience also made me reconsider what value defining terms like "plot" had in a close reading of literature. Had I not spent time doing that, I don't think the seminar would have been any less productive. In the future, I think I will frame the unit with Socratic Seminars to see if there is a qualitative difference in student comments and insights after the definition of terms and the group-led discussions.

Regarding the group assignment, the individual writing requirements were flat and unimaginative. Next time, I will have the group pose three essay questions and have each student respond to one of them.

So, even with the apparent "success" of this first Seminar, Rebolini's reflections provide a fine model of how performance assessments help teachers improve *their own* work to advance student learning. The Seminar's design, giving students the active role and responsibility, allow teachers to observe their class in action, to listen to how students think, to watch how they react to one another's comments and insights. With the help of a rubric like the one presented in Figure 4.8, assessment can be formalized and students can be given important feedback regarding their skills. Allowing students to self-assess, as Rebolini did in this assignment (and as many Socratic Seminar leaders do), also engages students actively in the assessment process and creates a platform for student/teacher conferences. Comparing student ratings and teacher evaluations from the same Seminar, perception checking and, more significantly, substantive conversations about student participation and teacher assessment design can occur.

Carlo Rebolini's introduction of Socratic Seminars at Garden City High School, provides a fine model for others to follow. The incremental steps, the careful explanation, the *inclusion* of the students in the "what" and "how" of the assessment process, are crucial steps for not only designing performance assessments but also for their successful implementation. In this case, the reaction of the students, their demonstration of what they learned, and the teacher's own insights into his teaching and curricular/assessment design, illustrate the usefulness of Socratic Seminars in broadening our assessment picture to include feedback in areas and on levels which traditional measures cannot.

TEACHING BASIC SKILLS WITH DEPTH

Margaret Metzger has been an outstanding classroom teacher at Brookline High School for many years. She has published widely, worked in the Teacher Education Department at Brown University, and has constantly pushed herself to learn more about the craft of teaching. In doing so, Margaret has adapted Socratic Seminars in a unique way, and provides still another example of how teachers can take the basic concepts behind performance assessments and redesign them to serve important ends in their classrooms.

In Metzger's case, she used Socratic Seminars to focus on a set of basic outcomes for students. Aside from learning to read in depth, Margaret believes it is important for teachers to gain insight into *how* students reach comprehension. She also finds that seminars can help unskilled readers work with difficult texts by focusing on complex sections of the book *first*, before reading the entire work. For more sophisticated readers, the reinforcement of in-depth reading is accomplished by examining a few lines of a particular reading closely — taking as much as an hour to discuss six lines of Dante or Shakespeare, for example. And for those students who are "non-academic," the Seminars serve to introduce them to the skills of discourse about textual material which we would like all our graduates to leave with. In sum, Margaret Metzger uses Socratic Seminars to accomplish a variety of basic skills for students and provide very important feedback to the teacher regarding student mastery of those skills.

An innovation Metzger has instituted in her Socratic Seminars changes the physical nature of the class and helps students focus on those basic skills which have been identified as the important outcomes for the group. Margaret's Socratic Seminars are arranged in two concentric circles — a "fishbowl" arrangement in which the inner circle comprises the Seminar discussants and the outer circle serves as observers. Both groups have important responsibilities toward the success of the Seminar.

While the inner circle has the responsibility of conducting the text-based discussion — presenting their comprehension and analytical skills — members of the outer circle are given particular assignments. Students in the outer circle are given specific students to monitor, or a specific skill to focus on, and must be prepared to report their findings in the debriefing. The outer group, then, becomes a critique circle, focusing on the *process* **and** content of the Socratic Seminar, while the inner circle is engaged in searching for the meaning in the text itself. All students have to prepare for the day's text, of course, since critiquing cannot occur in a vacuum and the observing group is expected to raise questions about the text which the inner circle may have missed.

Consider the implications of this innovation, particularly in relation to Metzger's outcomes. Whether the students will be in the inner or outer circle, all must do close reading of the text. Students in the inner circle are expected to respond to the opening question and carry the discussion, probing deeply for meaning, revealing their comprehension of the text, presenting their ability to articulate ideas, and so on. Those in the outer circle must listen carefully, observe the interplay of the inner circle, take notes, and provide insights not only about the discussion of the text but also about the process of the discussion — could this topic have been probed more deeply? Did the inner circle raise all the important issues connected to the text? Were there serious misreadings of the text, and if so, how and why? Consider the critical thinking skills those in the outer circle have to develop to provide effective feedback in the Seminar's debriefing. And consider how this innovation to the system can free the teacher to observe and assess students working on a wide range of skills in the context of one Seminar! The fact that Metzger also videotapes these performances and reviews them only adds to the power and effectiveness of this system.

Another important aspect of the Socratic Seminar system is that it occur on a regular basis, so that students have time to work on improving their skills, working toward mastery. The frequent use of Seminars also impresses upon students the value of the outcomes connected to the method. In Margaret Metzger's case, the Seminars are used again and again, with a wide variety of texts. Starting with the *Pledge of Allegiance* (the old standby), Metzger uses the Seminar to discuss Bradbury's *Fahrenheit 451*, the *Gettysburg Address*, the

"Preamble" to the *Constitution*, the last three pages of *The Great Gatsby*, a paragraph from *Walden* (starting with "I went to the woods because I wanted to live deliberately . . ."), a section from Cather's *My Antonia*, e.e. cummings's *america i love you*, and Langston Hughes's *Theme for English B*, to name a few. The point here is apparent — it is only through the regular use of this method that students will become comfortable and proficient with it. In Metzger's case, the innovation of the inner and outer circles increases the skills-work, above and beyond the textual examination, thereby broadening the assessment even further.

As a "final exam," Margaret Metzger's students engage in Socratic Seminars on Dante and Shakespeare. All the seminars are evaluated (and self-evaluated by students) according to a criteria developed by the students and the teacher. Metzger believes this system has increased her ability to assess student reading levels more clearly, because the students have to talk about what they've read in more than a superficial way. In her own words:

> For example, last week a student was discussing *Fahrenheit 451*, and assumed that Bradbury was against books. For the first time, I saw how completely this student could not work in abstract thinking — and irony and metaphor were incomprehensible to the student.

Consider how this observation will enable the teacher to work with that student — and to better understand the student's writing, too. Once again, we can see how performance assessments can provide information and feedback about student abilities which traditional assessments do not reveal.

Margaret Metzger's system for Socratic Seminars also broadens *our* view of how to implement performance assessments. It reinforces that there is no "one way" or "right" way to design or implement these assessments. What Margaret's example provides is an excellent illustration of how a teacher has carefully examined those skills and content outcomes, and identified not only which ones are most important, but also reflected upon what kinds of assessments will best help students achieve those outcomes. That kind of careful, reflective practice is one of the hallmarks of performance assessment design and implementation. It characterizes the departure from the traditional, linear curriculum → instruction → testing paradigm.

The new model, as exemplified by Metzger's innovation with Socratic Seminars, is one which examines carefully what it is we want students to know and be able to do in the skills, content, and disposition domains, *and then* decide what kinds of assessments will best inform instruction and direct curriculum selection to help students reach those outcomes. It requires a commitment to the goal of student learning, of course, which will break many established norms. It asks teachers to engage in reflective practice and cross-disciplinary conversations, destroying still more norms. But if student achievement and progress are our goals, can we demand any less? Examples like Margaret Metzger's point to how teachers can begin to move into new territory to promote more effective student learning.

USING SOCRATIC SEMINARS TO SHOW WHAT THEY KNOW

The Bronxville High School final Exhibition for 9th grade Western Civilization included a Socratic Seminar component. In reviewing that Exhibition, what we can see is still another way to use Socratic Seminar. Where the examples presented to this point have all engaged students in discussions *and then* asked them to write about what they had discussed, the Bronxville Exhibition did the opposite. Students spent time developing a rather complex piece of writing about literature, history, and art, connecting it to the Bosnian crisis of 1993, *and then* took part in a series of Socratic Seminars. The reasoning behind this is worth examining because it presents yet another variation of how to implement Socratic Seminars.

In reviewing the exit outcomes for Bronxville's 9th graders (Fig. 4.9), and reflecting on the Final Exhibition we were developing, the Interdisciplinary Team identified *seven* skills outcomes which a Socratic Seminar could assess: analytical reading, effective listening, working cooperatively in a group setting, speaking publicly, organization of materials, readings, etc., effective questioning, and group discussion. A number of content and attitude outcomes could also be met through the use of the Seminar method, so it was decided that it would be an appropriate assessment instrument. Students were familiar with the technique — so much so, in fact, that it was decided a student facilitator would be designated for each of the

FIGURE 4.9: BRONXVILLE HIGH SCHOOL — 9TH GRADE EXIT OUTCOMES

Exit Outcomes
9th Grade
Bil Johnson

Skills & Habits
- Research
- Writing in a variety of modes
- Analytical reading
- Working cooperatively in a group setting
- Working independently
- Effective listening
- Ability to speak publicly
- Effective time management
- Organization of materials, readings, etc.
- Good study habits
- Effective questioning
- Group discussion

Content
- The G.R.E.A.S.E.S. analytical model (Government, Religion, Economics, Art/Architecture, Science/Technology, Education, Social/Cultural Values) to understand cultures over time and geographic locations
- The foundations of Western Civilization, using the analytical model. Understanding where "we" (United States) come from.
- Basic cause-and-effect --- the flow of history as logical & predictable (if you know how to look)
- Art/architecutre appreciation
- Knowing primary/secondary sources
- Current events

Attitudes / Behaviors
- Responsible
- Open-minded
- Fair-minded
- Courteous, respectful
- Curiosity
- Reflective

Essential Questions
- How did we (the U.S.) get here?
- What is a good society/civilization?
- What is a fair or just society?
- What is a good citizen?

three Seminars and teachers would only provide the opening question and not even sit in the discussion circle.

Students were familiar with the Seminar rubric as well as with a "Daily Assessment" self-evaluation form (Fig. 4.10). What the teachers were hoping to observe was not only the connection between written student work but also the use of materials and references from work done throughout the year. What struck the teachers as most important was the creation of opening questions which would allow the students to genuinely show what they knew.

The hope was that engaging and inciting questions would set off a series of "knowledge reactions" in the students — causing them to begin making connections and building on each other's contributions with the material they had studied and written about. Could they make clear references to their work, support their claims with evidence, question each other with a challenging respect, and uncover even deeper meaning in the literary, historical, and artistic works we had studied? The team decided that Socratic Seminars were the way to find out.

The logistics for the Final Exhibition were in place: we would have 2 days with 94-minute blocks to discuss our work. A student facilitator would be designated (quite a few volunteered for the role) and the teachers would start the Seminar with a question. Three opening questions were developed and the plan was to spend about 1-hour on each. The only logistical glitch this presented is that the second Seminar would be interrupted because of the time factor. The team decided it would be worth running the risk of "flattening" out one discussion, hoping the students would rise to the occasion and be able to resurrect their energy and intensity a day later.

The opening questions were simple and proved wonderfully effective. Having decided to focus each Seminar along a discipline line, allowing students to bring in the connections (something we wanted to see them do without our prompting), the three questions were:

FIGURE 4.10: BRONXVILLE HIGH SCHOOL — DAILY ASSESSMENT

Socratic Seminar Assessment Criteria

5=Excellent

    a. Number of comments (active participation, pt.1)
       A "5" would require a number of timely and appropriate comments, not simply a quantity of remarks.

    b. Quality of Comments
       Comments would be thoughtful and reflective; they would respond respectfully to other students' remarks. They would provoke other questions and comments from the group.

    c. Text Reference
       Student would make clear reference to the text being discussed AND would connect it to other texts or reference points from previous readings and discussions.

    d. Listens to others (active participation, pt.2)
       The student's posture, demeanor, behavior clearly respects respect and attentiveness to others. Responses to others based on their comments would be a clear indicator of "5" behavior in this category.

    e. Involved in the text; prepared for discussion
       Student would have notes and text references (or questions based on the text) prepared for class and ready at the beginning of the discussion.

4=Good

    a. Number of Comments (active participation, pt.1)
       Student would volunteer comments without being asked, most would be appropriate and reflect some thoughtfulness.

    b. Quality of Comments
       Comments would indicate the student has given some thought to the text. They would lead to other questions or remarks from the student (if not from others).

    c. Text Reference
       Discussion would indicate student has done the reading with some thoroughness, although it would lack a certain eye for detail or critical insight. (Doesn't recognize symbols, or ignores charts/graphs, etc.)

    d. Listens to others (active participation, pt.2)
       While listening to others *most* of the time, student does not stay focused on other's comments (too busy formulating his/her own) or loses continuity of discussion. Shows some consistency in responding to the comments of others.

    e. Involved with the Material/Prepared for class
       There is some indication of preparation --- some notes or text underlining; more than a passing acquaintance with the materials for the discussion so the day's discussion is not delayed by lack of preparation.

3=Satisfactory
a. Number of Comments (active participation, pt.1)
   The student struggles, but DOES participate and occasionally
   offers a comment, though most remarks must be elicted.
b. Quality of Comments
   Comments react "in the moment" and show little thoughtfulness
   or reflection. There are almost no comments in reaction to
   other students' comments.
c. Text Reference
   Student may have done the reading but there is little
   indication of it based on few or no notes or little or no
   text underlining.
d. Listens to others (active participation, pt.2)
   While there is an occasional direct response to
   others, student generally is only politely attentive,
   seldom contributing to the discussion.
e. Involved with the Material/Prepared for discussion
   While the student has done the reading, there is little
   to indicate any reflective thought or preparation has
   occurred before discussion begins.

2= Minimally Satisfactory
a. Number of comments (active participation, pt.1)
   Student minimally participates, only responds to direct
   questions and even then is minimal in responding.
b. Quality of Comments
   Comments simply restate a question or point previously
   raised and add nothing new to the discussion or provoke
   no responses or questions.
c. Text Reference
   Student clearly has NOT read the entire text and cannot
   sustain any reference to it in the course of discussion.
d. Listens to others (active participation, pt. 2)
   Student "drifts" in and out of discussion, listening
   to some remarks while clearly missing or ignoring others.
e. Involved with the Material/Prepared for Discussion
   Other than showing up with the necessary materials for
   class -- the text, paper for note-taking, etc. --- student
   shows minimal preparation or involvement with his/her work.

1= Unsatifactory
a. Number of Comments (active participation, pt.1)
   Student does not participate and/or only makes negative
   or disruptive remarks.
b. Quality of Comments
   Student's comments are inappropriate or off the topic.
c. Text Reference
   Student is unable to refer to text for evidence or support
   of his remarks or others.
d. Listens to others (active participation, pt.2)
   Student is clearly disrespectful of others when they
   are speaking; behavior indicates total non-invovlement
   with the group or discussion.
e. Involved with material/Prepared for class
   Student is clearly NOT prepared for class. NO indication of preparation.

- What if Shakespeare were writing today — how would he portray the Bosnian crisis in a play?

- If Picasso were to paint "Guernica" in 1993, what do you think it would look like?

- If the morning news said Middle-Eastern Muslims were going to begin arming the Bosnian Muslims, what advice should President Clinton be given?

The results of these Seminars surpassed our wildest expectations. Not only were the discussions lively and heated, but students consistently brought in references to works they had studied throughout the year. As we observed, discussions began with simple "brainstorming" ideas — would Shakespeare use a format like *Romeo and Juliet*, would Picasso have to use colors to portray the bloody Bosnian crisis, would Clinton have to consult with the United Nations first — but quickly escalated into animated exchanges referring to the *Melian Dialogues*, how Alexander the Great attempted to mix cultures after his conquests, the concepts of heroism as portrayed in the *Odyssey*, and so on. In fact, the students were so engaged in the discussion (our concern about the divided Seminar proved unfounded) that when we stopped the class with 5 minutes left — so that we could wrap up the discussion and do our final "house-keeping" for the semester — we were met with howls of protest: "I still have something to say!" "I didn't get a chance to respond to Chris's statement!" What made this all the more striking to us was that this was the *last day of classes for the year!* These students had 47 minutes left in their freshman year in high school and they were upset that their teachers were making them stop working. From a teachers' perspective, this was a dream come true.

Not all Socratic Seminars may have the kind of results elicited from the Bronxville Exhibition, but it should be pointed out that this was a heterogeneously grouped class which simply had experience with Seminar discussions and had comments of substance to make. They were invested in their work and believed the discussions had genuine relevance. We were able to clearly observe direct connections between student work and their thinking in the Seminar discussion, affording us a much clearer picture of our own progress with the interdisciplinary program.

The Socratic Seminar, combined with the written assignment (Fig. 4.11), proved to be an extremely effective way to assess the exit outcomes we had identified in September. It allowed the teachers to see where students had progressed to in relation to those outcomes, allowing for a more accurate assessment of student progress. Because this group had also kept portfolios throughout the year, the days following the Seminars were spent reviewing student work, not only from the Final Exhibition, but also in relation to the evidence which had been accumulated throughout the school year on each student. This provided a broad view of student achievement in areas of reading, writing speaking, and listening skills, critical thinking skills, content domain objectives, and progress toward attitude/behavior outcomes. The Socratic Seminar did not reveal all of this, of course, but without it we would not have had as broad or as clear a picture of what our students had truly accomplished during the year.

SOCRATIC SEMINARS AND ASSESSMENT SYSTEMS

The variety of Socratic Seminars presented here are intended to provide classroom practitioners with another method for assessing students which provides valuable feedback about student progress and achievement. It is recommended that Mortimer Adler's books be read and some form of training be done before implementing Seminars, but, even more importantly, that teachers engage in discussions about how this method would help to better reveal those aspects of student thinking and learning which their present system may not tap into.

In the cases presented here, Socratic Seminars are one part of a larger performance assessment system — and that is important to note. None of the performance assessments in this book are "stand-alone" systems. As mentioned in the final example from Bronxville, students had been involved in performances and Exhibitions, collecting and presenting their work in student portfolios, and *had* engaged in Socratic Seminars during the school year, before participating in the final Seminar as part of an Exit Exhibition. This system did not spring full-blown from the head of Zeus. It was the result of 4 or 5 years of teachers working together to implement a broader range of assessments to better know the progress of their students. Each of the other schools presented would offer similar stories.

FIGURE 4.11: BRONXVILLE HIGH SCHOOL — 9TH GRADE FINAL

9th Grade Final
A/B Interdisc
June, 1993

PART ONE

Students will choose one character from each column and write a short paper considering how each would advise President Clinton on the Bosnian situation. In writing the paper students should consider the following issues:
- short & long term effects
- reactions at home & abroad
- negotiating with allies
- United Nations role
- potential gains & losses: human, economic, spiritual terms
- military & political considerations: bombing, quarantines, embargoes, No-Fly zones, sanctions, war crimes, sending in troops
- the role of women - in combat & other capacities

Beyond interpreting the specific character's advice to Clinton, students should use references to other works they have studied this semester.

The Characters (students may include others)

Literature	*Art*	*History*
Odysseus	Maya Lin	Alexander the Great
Emmet	Goya	Punic Wars
Penelope	Picasso	Persian Wars
Tybalt	Delacroix	Charlemagne
Juliet	Greek Vase (Euphronius)	Machiavelli
Lysistrata	Van Eyck	Pax Romana
Sam		Feudal Warrior/Crusades
		The Melian Dialogue

PART TWO
SOCRATIC SEMINAR

Students will be presented with a scenario related to the Bosnian crisis (not necessarily a factual one; it could be a "what if . . .") and have to engage in a critical discussion in which they apply their work from PART ONE, as well as their work from the semester.

Final Exhibition Preparation
A/B Interdisc

The Problem you will be faced with:
You will be asked to respond to a simple task ---- cooling down one of the world's hottest spots! The Bosnian Conflict is clearly out of control and no one seems to know what to do. So, you are going to help. Based on your knowledge of literature, history, and art, you are going to prepare position papers which will advise the U.S. government on what course of action it needs to take to help resolve the Bosnian Crisis.

The Process you will follow:
You will need to read/review various sources you have read/studied this year, or have been given in the last few weeks. Based on those sources/readings, etc. you will devise a position which you believe the U.S. should take on the Bosnian crisis ---- *from the point of view of the* **SOURCE** (whether it's an author, a figure from history, an artist, whomever)! You will cite *specific textual evidence*   to support your position. In all, you will write three in-class position statements (one English source, one Social Studies source, one Art source) over three days (probably June 9,10,11).

READINGS FOR BOSNIAN CRISIS

You will receive a packet of readings about the Bosnian Crisis. You must read **ALL** of the packet in order to be prepared to write an intelligent essay from any point of view, and to participate in the Class Discussion/Seminar (Part Two of the Final Exhibition on June 14 & 15).

Part Two of the Exhibition
You will be expected to articulately express advice to the U.S. government as to what its course of action in the Bosnian Crisis should be from **TWO (or more)** points of view: a) the point of view of historical (and/or literary &/or artistic) figures;
        b) your own point of view.

All points of view must be supported by **FACTUAL EVIDENCE & LOGICAL INFERENCE!**

The development of performance assessment systems is a developmental, thoughtful process — these are not "substitutes" for present testing measures and are not intended to simply be "put in" where we used to give a unit test. Focusing on what it is we want to know that students have learned, and how it is we want to see students exhibit their learning, is a key first step in the process. Again, this is not intended to present performance assessments in an "either/or" context. The intent here is to help teachers create assessment systems which provide feedback to students about their progress and to teachers about the effectiveness of their instructional programs. So, if we believe intelligent intellectual discourse is an important outcome for our students, and if we are going to assign grades for "class participation" and "discussion skills," Socratic Seminars may well be a method which allows us to better achieve those ends.

Grading students for Socratic Seminars, and for any of the other performance assessments presented here, can be problematic, of course. It raises the issues of standards, criteria, and scoring rubrics. Throughout the earlier chapters, many of the assessments were presented with rubrics — as have the Socratic Seminars here. It was mentioned that some of these rubrics have flaws and there is no "one, right" rubric for scoring performance assessments. Nonetheless, these are important elements of performance assessment systems and need as much care and thought as the assessments themselves. Developing rubrics which represent the standards and criteria which exemplify the student outcomes we value, then, is the next task teachers must undertake as we move further into the lightly trod paths of the territory ahead.

5

STANDARDS, CRITERIA, AND RUBRICS: INCLUDING TEACHERS AND STUDENTS IN THE SEARCH FOR QUALITY

standard: An acknowledged measure of comparison for quantitative or qualitative value; A degree or level of requirement, excellence, or attainment.

The American Heritage Dictionary

The nation is rife with arguments and debates over *standards*. Every professional organization representing teachers in each discrete discipline has, or is in the process of, churning out *standards* for classroom practitioners. National panels, state commissions, union representatives, and self-appointed "experts" are all presenting the public with *standards*. Is it sound and fury signifying nothing — or is this an important conversation which teachers *need to be a part of*?

The fact is, practicing teachers and their students are seldom invited to join these conversations, much less to serve on the boards, panels, or commissions which ultimately issue *the* "standards." We are left with a melange of ideas, concepts, prescriptions, and possible requirements which will be foisted on those who have had the least input, but potentially possess, along with local parents, the most knowledge about the issue.

And, amid all the hew and cry about *standards*, the issue of quality seldom surfaces. When these organizations present their standards, are they telling us these are standards of excellence or merely "acceptable" standards? All of this has implications for teachers and students, of course, and is inextricably woven into the concept of performance assessment. Because performance assessments are ultimately geared toward *performance*, teachers and students must be **totally clear** as to what performance standards for excellence, acceptability, or reworking are.

The history and legacy of testing in this country is one of internally subjective and externally arbitrary evaluation of student work. Do any two teachers in the *same* department in the *same* school give *the same* "B" or "A?" If not, what is an "A" or "B" in that school worth? What is the *standard* for "A" or "B" work? And who decides? And by what process? And how does the student know? These are important questions which are seldom raised. Because so much, in terms of student "success," is determined by external test results (SATs, Regents exams, Metropolitan Reading exams, etc.), no culture has emerged in schools about standards or quality. It is only in the last decade, since the school restructuring movement has gained momentum, that discussions about standards and quality have become issues for debate. That debate, however, has been controlled by external agencies, often far from the classroom. In moving to performance assessments, teachers can, and must, bring the discussion about standards and quality to the forefront in their schools. As with so many issues present in the world of the '90s, the standards and quality debate is one in which *teachers and students* can think globally and act locally, with genuine impact.

The inherent problems revolving around the standards issue as it exists today are these:

- ♦ What is the purpose for setting standards — and who makes that decision?

- ♦ Where does the question of quality emerge in the standards debate — and how will that conversation be framed?

- ♦ How do parents and students know what the standards are in their school — and how are those standards implemented?

Before specifically discussing standards, anyone involved in such a conversation must be clear as to what "standards" truly represent. Ultimately, "standards" are about *accountability*. They create the yardstick by which we measure the accomplishment of our students and our educational programs. Have we met the "standards" of the State, of ETS, and so on? The primary problem with the current system is that the standards by which schools and students are measured are detached and arbitrary systems inflicted upon the local community. The strongest advocates for performance assessments have made compelling arguments enumerating the changes which need to occur if we are to develop systems which are genuinely *accountable,* with clear and known standards where they will have the greatest impact — in the individual classrooms and schools of this nation. The challenge to develop local standards which focus on *the quality of student work*, then, is one of the key aspects of developing an performance assessment system. As with so much of the work with performance assessments, this requires a radical shift in school norms.

DEVELOPING LOCAL STANDARDS FOR QUALITY STUDENT WORK

Several embedded norms have to shift if we are to develop useful and credible standards and systems of genuine accountability in schools.

♦ Teacher isolation, working in cellular classrooms and having little contact or conversation with other teachers, must stop.

♦ Administrators must become *facilitators of opportunity* to insure that teachers have common time to meet around meaningful agendas which focus on student work.

♦ School boards and communities, administrators and teachers, must publicly discuss the **meaning** of standardized tests and seriously consider whether these instruments provide **useful feedback** about authentic teaching and learning in their community.

♦ Students must be invited to join these conversations to learn to reflect on the *meaning* of their schooling. This has to "make sense" to the students or it will simply be another exercise in which the adults of the community impose mandates and structures on students, resulting in young people going through motions which make little or no sense to them.

Crucial to all these conversations is clearly understanding what it is we want our students to leave our school systems with. So, not only must we be clear about what it is we want our students to know and be able to do, but we must also be equally clear about what the standards are for achievement. And those standards must then serve as the accountability measure for our schools.

In *Assessing Student Performance* (Jossey-Bass, 1993), Grant Wiggins has made a strong case for implementing performance assessment systems which build *accountability* into their standards for achievement. In no uncertain tones, Wiggins characterizes the present system this way:

Too many teachers and administrators are in the habit of accepting praise for student success while explaining why student failure is not their fault. . . . In the absence of an accountability system that would make teachers worry more about the effects of their teaching than the intent, many educators still do not understand their jobs: many wrongly come to think that their purpose is to teach what they know and like, on a relatively fixed schedule — *irrespective of the learning that does or does not ensue. . . .* In short, teachers are not now obligated, either by job description or direct pressures on the institution by other institutions, to *really* know how they are doing and to do something about it when things go badly.

Assessing Student Performance, p. 276

It is important to note here that Wiggins is not teacher-bashing. He is effectively describing the culture which exists in most schools. In the absence of clearly defined local standards which schools and teachers are held accountable to, educators consistently mistake intent for effect. And this is the point at which performance assessment implementation *has to* attack the existing norms of schools, bringing about authentic change aimed at producing quality student work geared toward high standards.

In *Graduation by Exhibition* (ASCD, 1993), Joseph McDonald states, "Schools wrestling with standards typically begin by building internal mechanisms for teachers to talk with one another about the quality of student work"(p. 55). This starting point speaks to the first changed norm which *must* occur if we are do develop meaningful standards in our schools. Wiggins likens it to a coaching staff whose team is 0 and 6 at midseason. Because their goals are known, because standards of (athletic) performance are clear, such a staff would *have to* reassess its approach and make adjustments so the team's success would improve (*Assessing Student Performance,* p. 277). Nothing like this occurs in schools today because teachers — even teachers in the same department — have little or no idea what anyone else does, much less what the quality of student work is! As Wiggins points out "How many middle schools require that their faculty spend a day with high school faculty to learn how well or poorly their former students have been prepared?"or "How many high schools organize focus groups of college professors to find out how their syllabi, assignments, and tests are viewed?" (p. 266) The examples, at present, are few and far between. Yet, if we are to establish genuine standards and build in real accountability, such practices *must* begin to emerge. And this is where another norm must change.

Administrators can no longer conceive of schools as hierarchical bureaucracies with a top-down management structure. With the advent of performance assessment systems, it is incumbent upon administrators to become *facilitators of opportunities* for teachers. While sounding the call and providing some vision for higher standards and accountability, administrators must be inventive and creative in finding ways for teachers to meet and discuss what their school's standards are — and how teachers will be held accountable for helping students meet those standards. There **are** ways to do this, even in traditional and rigidly structured schools. "Stealing time" for teachers may be the greatest challenge administrators face in shifting the culture of their schools, but it can be done. Imagine the difference in school culture if faculty meetings were considered Workshops or Work Sessions focused on developing standards, rather than administrative meetings about hall duty and detention? How much of what occurs in most faculty meetings could be accomplished through simple memos to staff, saving valuable time for real work for teachers?

What if periods were shortened by 3–5 minutes each on the day of a faculty meeting, creating an additional half to three-quarters of an hour for teachers to meet to focus on the serious work of developing standards? What if administrators and Guidance Counselors offered to "cover" classes for a group of teachers for half a day, allowing those teachers to meet for discussions about standards and accountability? These are not impossible proposals which "can't happen." Almost any administrator could use these mechanisms and others to find time for teachers to meet to discuss standards in their school.

In the same way, any standards conversation must begin by looking at how we gauge our standards at present. Often, SAT or other external, standardized tests are the only measure. Have people from the community, the school board, and the schools themselves ever sat down and discussed whether this is a useful measure of student achievement? Are these the standards to which we hold our students? Since students never know which questions they got right or wrong, how can a culture of student progress toward the achievement of standards be created around such measures? If these conversations are not broached, it is unlikely any school can develop authentic standards or provide suitable accountability for its work.

And what of the students themselves? At present, students have little or no voice or choice in schools. This is not to say, as was characterized to me by a colleague once, that we need to "turn the asylum over to the inmates," but to ask whether teachers are, in fact, coordinating intent and effect. As Wiggins cogently notes:

> We are still light-years away from treating students as clients seeking a service — clients who are able to seek and receive change in the (daily) service when the methods used and prescriptions made by teachers fail to help them. . . . It is almost unheard of for teachers to have their ineffective methods challenged, their questionable grades overturned, or their classroom duties altered because of a failure to serve the clients well. . . . The voice option is the only way in which dissatisfied customers or members can react. . . .

> *Assessing Student Performance*, p. 263

His proposals for creating greater student voice may seem radical, but they are simply outside the bounds of the present norms. If we are to begin to engage in serious conversations about developing standards and systems of accountability which are genuinely effective, we might do well to consider Wiggins's ideas.

> The primary "unit" of accountability is the *particular* set of teachers and administrators that are *directly* responsible for each child's experience and achievement. . . . Schools would thus be instantly more accountable if we worried less about arcane psychometric proxy tests and worried more about making the teacher's daily work public and giving the student performer a more powerful voice. . . . . What if each teacher had to display monthly the best work from *each* student in a public place in school? . . . What if performance appraisals were centered on teacher self-assessment in reference to a range of student work from a major assignment? These are the kinds of mechanisms which would improve accountability immediately and forcefully.

> *Assessing Student Performance*, p. 264

While these suggestions depart from present practice, consider how they bring together the "norm-breaking" which is proposed here. Teachers participating in this type of system would *have to* talk to each other about the student work and range of assignments displayed. Administrators would *have to* facilitate the creation of an atmosphere where teachers would be *encouraged and rewarded* for participating. Students would gain a powerful voice in a public forum, being able to examine their work next to others, as well as examine the work of their teachers, engendering conversations about "what works" and "what doesn't," thereby improving the quality of the educational program. Most significantly, this entire approach makes public the issue of standards and accountability — thereby helping everyone focus on what is most important about teaching and learning, the student's progress.

This is not a discussion about "Standards — How To." It is a provocation for teachers, students, administrators, parents, and school boards. What *are* your standards? How are they determined and how do they, in turn, determine accountability for students and teachers? The suggestions here call for a new way to approach the issue; a way which defies the norms which currently exist in most schools. Giving greater voice to those closest to the work — the students and teachers — and asking other members of the Learning Community to enter the conversation — these suggestions represent an outline of how to *begin* the conversation. At present, schools have no standards. The variance of what a grade is worth from one classroom to the next is mind boggling. Until the serious conversations begin, until teachers are given the time to meet and talk, until parents and administrators support and facilitate these conversations, and until students are consulted as part of the process, we will continue to swim in very murky waters arbitrarily labeled "standards." This is a process, not an event, and it is a process which is a logical and integral part of developing an performance assessment system. For the classroom teacher, an entry point which is equally significant to performance assessments and easily accessible to classroom practice, is criteria and rubrics.

DEVELOPING RUBRICS AND SCORING CRITERIA
TO DEFINE STANDARDS

Rubric: Any brief, authoritative rule or direction.

Criterion: A standard, rule, or test on which a judgment or decision can be based.

The American Heritage Dictionary

Translating standards into classroom application can occur through the development and use of rubrics and scoring criteria. In its ecclesiastical definition, a "rubric" was a direction or set of instructions, generally printed in red (its meaning in Latin), explaining how liturgical services were to be rendered. In essence, rubrics were instructions or guidelines which explained how a performance should be properly presented. In classroom terms, a rubric is a guideline for determining how well students are performing any number of tasks in relation to the standards of the school. It is, most commonly, a scoring device which allows a judge (a teacher or other audience) to distinguish how effectively students are performing assigned tasks.

Criteria are those descriptors or indicators which clarify for both performers and audience what is required to succeed at certain tasks. For example, the criteria for pole-vaulting involves, first and foremost, clearing the crossbar without knocking it off the stanchions. Other criteria might describe mechanical procedures, like how the pole should be held, the length of the approach track, the speed recommended for the vaulter, the proper placement of the pole on the ground, and so on. Criteria, in Grant Wiggins's words, "involve the conditions that any performance must meet to be successful; they define, operationally, what meeting the task requirements means" ("What is a Rubric?" **C.L.A.S.S.** document, 1994, p. 3). So, one criterion for hitting a home run in baseball is that the ball must clear the fence in fair territory between the left field and right field foul poles.

Here we begin to see where rubrics and standards intersect with the notion of criteria. A Little League home run will greatly differ from one hit at Yankee Stadium — but the criteria remains the same. The standard is *equivalent*, though **not** equal — the performer must be able to achieve a feat which requires uncommon strength and timing. The *ultimate* standard of excellence and achievement might be hitting the ball out of Yankee Stadium, but we adjust our standards and rubrics so that performers from novice through expert levels can be judged as to how well they meet the criteria *at their level*.

To use a more academic example: students are capable of identifying **excellent** writing. If asked, they can bring in an example of writing they believe is excellent and they can defend it. In that defense, they will identify characteristics — indicators — of excellent writing. Many of these will be basic criteria which apply to *any* writing, no matter what level the performer is at. Very often students (and teachers) identify writing criteria related to *mechanics, organization, content, sentence structure,* and *vocabulary*. Certainly, these are important criteria for writing, but they speak to one of the most significant problems which surrounds the standards–rubric–criteria discussion. That is, do any of the listed writing criteria reflect any aspect of the *quality* of the writing being judged? In other words, a totally bland, uninteresting, poorly documented piece of writing could, in fact, score fairly well if those were the only criteria used. *This is where our search for standards intersects with rubrics and scoring criteria and opens the door for classroom teachers to begin these conversations with their students.*

TEASING OUT QUALITY THROUGH RUBRIC DESIGN

Throughout the earlier chapters, examples of performance assessments often included rubrics and scoring criteria — and statements were made as to how those rubrics and criteria were, in some way, flawed. The remainder of this chapter will be aimed at presenting rubrics and criteria to analyze the strengths and weaknesses in what we present as guidelines to student performance. Embedded in such analysis is the question of standards and quality. As has been mentioned before, even if the rubrics and scoring criteria accompanying a performance assessment are not "perfect," they are still a marked improvement over what has gone before — students working in a total vacuum regarding what the expectations for quality work might be other than an individual teacher's subjective, idiosyncratic judgment.

What follows then, is a careful look at four examples of rubrics and scoring criteria to see what we can learn about standards and quality and how we can best develop meaningful instruments to evaluate student work. The format for each investigation is the same: we consider *"what works," "what doesn't,"* and what are the *implications for standards and quality*. Between the examples and the discussion of each, some sense of how one might develop a comparable system for individual classrooms should emerge.

THE PIERRE VAN CORTLANDT MIDDLE SCHOOL NEWSPAPER PROJECT

WHAT WORKS

Rick Casey's newspaper project for his middle schoolers in Croton-on-Hudson, makes it clear that **Work Habits, Research,** and **Presentation** (Fig. 5.1) are the focus of the assessment. Within those categories we can tease out the important standards:

- ◆ Meeting deadlines; using class time effectively.
- ◆ Thorough research of content.
- ◆ Attention to detail regarding writing mechanics and appearance.

If you were a middle schooler engaged in this project, it should be clear to you what the expectations for success are.

WHAT DOESN'T

As with so many first-generation rubrics and scoring criteria, the focus of attention here is on mechanics, observation of student industry, and "good citizenship" (meeting deadlines). It is difficult to nail down what we consider *high quality* work in written terms and, in fact, until student work is collected and examined, students cannot be presented with clear examples of what we mean. As mentioned earlier, students could achieve "E" ratings for their work on this project *without* producing a newspaper which was particularly interesting to read! It could have all the facts right, all deadlines met, and it could *look* wonderful (thanks to students knowing how to manipulate a good graphics software program) *without* achieving a level of writing which was memorable, or engaging, or of particularly good quality.

FIGURE 5.1: VAN CORTLANDT MIDDLE SCHOOL — NEWSPAPER PROJECT GRADING CRITERIA

American Revolutionary Newspaper
Grading Criteria

Although you may elect to complete this project working in a group of 1-3 students, each student will be graded individually. Students will receive separate grades for each of the criteria below:

Work Habits
Students will be given a considerable amount of class time for research, drafting and word processing of information. In order to ensure that students do not fall behind in their work, they will have to produce one finalized written piece every other day.

E - Student meets all deadlines; observation indicates that student consistently uses class time toward completion of this assignment.

G - Student fails to meet 1-2 deadlines, but shows consistent, daily progress toward completion of this project. Student consistently uses class time toward completion of the assignment.

S - Student fails to meet 1-2 deadlines. Progress is inconsistent, but noticeable. Student uses class time only when directed to do so.

N - Student fails to meet 3 or more deadlines. Student fails to complete all required parts of the newspaper. Student fails to use class time despite teacher prompting.

Research
Each of the 7 pieces of this assignment should show student research into the events of the American Revolutionary period.

E - Articles indicate a thorough and accurate understanding of the events and issues of the Revolutionary era. No gaps or misstatements in content are noted.

G - Articles indicate a clear grasp of the events and issues of the period, however, some minor gaps or misstatements are noted.

S - Articles indicate only a cursory or superficial understanding of the events and issues being reported. Some serious gaps a/o misstatements are noted.

N - Articles indicate no understanding of the issues and events of the period. Articles lack important information a/o contain numerous misstatements of fact.

Presentation
Newspapers should be pleasing to the eye, and be "reader-friendly". Articles should be proofread and be free of spelling, grammatical and mechanical errors. Articles continued on another page should be clearly marked.

E - Newspaper shows careful planning and a consistent format. Graphics are included. Newspaper has obviously been proofread for errors. All components, including headlines, by-lines and datelines are noted. All requirements are met.

G - Articles are generally free of spelling and grammatical errors. All components are noted. All requirements are met. Graphics are included.

S - Articles are generally free of spelling and grammatical errors. One or more components have been omitted. One or two requirements have not been met. Graphics are included.

N - Articles contain numerous spelling and grammatical errors. Layout is inconsistent. Numerous components are missing. More than two requirements are missing. No graphics are included.

IMPLICATIONS FOR STANDARDS AND QUALITY

The obvious implication regarding this grading criteria is that the next generation of it needs to pay more attention to quality — particularly regarding writing. Because examples would now exist (those newspapers produced by this group), teachers and students will be able to identify what quality writing for this project might be and the rubric can be revised accordingly. The conversation students and teachers have about that revision is the most important implication regarding the development of standards.

THE FULTON VALLEY PREP/PINER HIGH SCHOOL SCIENCE FAIR RUBRIC

WHAT WORKS

First and foremost, the classifications of **Mastery** and **Distinguished** indicate levels of achievement for which students should aspire (Fig. 5.2). In that sense, the message sent to students is that nothing less is really acceptable and that students are being held to high expectations. The rubric is clear in its requirements:

- ♦ Students are expected to show their *process* of development.
- ♦ A substantial *amount* of work is expected to be placed on display.
- ♦ Attention to an understanding of Newtonian Physics is expected.
- ♦ There is a definite value on group cooperation stressed.

WHAT DOESN'T

One of the most difficult problems with developing rubrics and scoring criteria is **language**. While terms might be explained and discussed, with examples, in class, questions still arise as to the real *meaning* of terms used in a rubric like this. What is "striking" or "attractive?" *How much* "attention to detail" is "careful?" What does an "in-depth summary" look like compared to one without depth? In the same way, *how* do conclusions reveal "thoughtful and significant insight?"

FIGURE 5.2: FULTON VALLEY PREP/PINER HIGH SCHOOL — SCIENCE FAIR RUBRIC

Sciences Core
The Physics of Sports and Recreation

Fulton
Valley
Prep

Rubric for Science Fair Projects

Mastery:	Distinguished:
1. Display Board clearly reflects the product development process.	Overall: Display Board is striking, attractive, well-organized, thorough and shows careful attention to detail.
2. Display Board includes summaries of all experiments and the results, with appropriate illustrations, measurements, calculations, and graphs.	1. See *Mastery*.
3. Display Board includes a model or drawing of the final product.	2. See *Mastery*. Also, neatly written, thorough, in-depth summaries of experiments, including quantative data, measurements, calculations and graphs.
4. Display Board includes writeup with appropriate conclusions based on data.	3. See *Mastery*. Also, model or drawing is to scale, neat, clearly labelled, and detailed.
5. Display Board includes thorough explanation of the relevance of the principles of Newtonian physics to the performance of the product.	4. See *Mastery*. Also, conclusions show thoughtful and significant insight into the experimental results and data.
6. Notebook is a thorough record of the process of the development of the final product, including lab writeups, answers to assigned questions, vocabulary exercises, and reflective writings about the concepts, experiments and results.	5. See *Mastery*. Also shows clear connections between the performance of the product and the Newtonian principles involved.
7. Product exhibits care in thought, planning, and construction. Attention to detail is evident.	6. See *Mastery*. Notebook entries are thoughtful and in-depth and reflect clear insight into the connections between the experiments, readings, and concepts.
	7. See *Mastery*. Product also shows originality and creativity.

It is easy to pick on the vocabulary used in a rubric or scoring criteria, but it is a highly significant point to focus on. Again, without examples of prior student work — whether in writing or on video- or audiotape, or in some other medium — it is extremely difficult for students to know what we mean when we use terms like these.

IMPLICATIONS

One possible solution, or at least a strategy, is to present students with a rubric like this, conduct a discussion *about the terms in question*, and record the examples which arise *from the class*. Those examples then become **part** of the final rubric which students will use in developing their projects. In this way, the scoring criteria becomes more clear to the students, and the standards which we are aiming for begin to flesh themselves out for students and teachers.

The Fulton Valley Prep example is a good one to include among our models because it presents an uncompromising approach to the *level of achievement* we can set for our students. While we must always gauge whether our students are ready for Yankee Stadium, it never hurts to consider setting the crossbar at a challenging height and demanding the stretch for excellence, while always building a safety net for repeated attempts at improvement.

FULTON VALLEY PREP/PINER HIGH SCHOOL HEROES EXHIBITION RUBRIC

WHAT WORKS

The refinement of the Science Fair rubric we witness here, is the creation of categories for "Project Content," "Project Format," and "Defense" (Fig. 5.3). Again, consider what this *immediately* tells students — there is an expectation regarding content, there is a standard regarding format, there *will be* an oral defense of the project. There are some basic expectations articulated in the rubric as well: a research component including a bibliography; a written presentation based on a proscribed format; neatness, graphics, and a variety of presentational modes; an oral component which encourages well-rehearsed and articulate presentation, ready to field questions about the work.

HEROES Exhibition

A Collection of Heroes
Rubric

	Mastery (B)	Distinguished (A)
PROJECT CONTENT	1. The project contains a clear, thoughtful definition of a hero for our society.	1. The project contains a clear, thoughtful, multi-faceted definition of a hero for our society.
	2. The project includes a collection of heroes who fit the author's definition.	2. The project includes a varied collection of heroes who fit the author's definition.
	3. Each hero in the collection is described accurately and connections between the heroes and the definition are evident.	3. Each hero in the collection is described accurately and in detail and connections between the heroes and the definition are clearly drawn .
	4. The author has researched the heroes in the collection and has included a bibliography of sources.	4. The author has thoroughly researched the heroes in the collection and has included a bibliography of sources.

Note: The size of the collection (number of heroes) should be related both to the choice of format and the depth of descriptions. E.g. a calendar would show 12 heroes and trading cards probably 12-15, while a speech or monologue series would present 3-4 heroes in greater depth.

PROJECT FORMAT	1. Written material is the original creation of the author or is clearly labeled as a quotation with the source identified. 2. Written materials are organized and readable, with an introduction, body and conclusion. Hypercard stacks allow easy travel among cards. 3. Written materials are neatly hand-written in ink or typed and contain few spelling, punctuation or usage errors. 4. The layout and graphics in an anthology, calendar, cards, magazine or mural are neat and easy to follow. 5. The performer (series of monologues or speech) speaks clearly and loudly and, although using a script, shows evidence of ample rehearsal.	1. Written material is the original creation of the author or is clearly labeled as a quotation with the source identified. 2. Written materials are well-organized and interesting, with an introduction, body and conclusion. Hypercard stacks allow easy travel among cards and use graphics and backgrounds creatively. 3. Written materials are typed and contain minimal spelling, punctuation or usage errors. 4. The layout and graphics in an anthology, calendar, cards, magazine or mural are creative, eye-catching and professional-looking. 5. The performer (series of monologues or speech) speaks clearly and loudly and has memorized the material, referring minimally to note cards. The presentation is energetic, believable and convincing.
DEFENSE	1. The presenter can explain reasons for his/her definition and can field questions about the heroes in the collection.	1. The presenter can explain connections between his/her definition and our society and can thoroughly defend her/his choice of heroes for the collection.

WHAT DOESN'T

In general this is an effective rubric which suffers from the same problems as the earlier ones — terminology and the question of quality. And, again, in the absence of specific examples of student work, it might be hard for students to understand what constitutes a product which is "creative, eye-catching, and professional-looking."

Once again the issue of quality has to be raised, too. If the expectation is "professional-looking" work, should it be compared to a magazine we purchase on a newsstand? If so, then which one? What is the baseline for quality here? Is it previous student work — that is, earlier work by these particular students, or work done by students from previous classes?

IMPLICATIONS

The problem raised by the quality issue is the difficult one and speaks directly to the standards question. On what basis are we gauging the quality of our students' work? What are the benchmarks? What are the "anchors" of high quality (a Grant Wiggins term) against which student *know* their work will be judged? What will the assessors use to compare this work to? What is fair, yet still high quality? How much weight do we give to the *progress* students have made since they began the class? Do we consider *effort*, even if the quality is poor? These are not simple questions to answer and this is not meant to denigrate the Fulton Valley Prep work. Again, we are looking at first-generation attempts at establishing standards and making evaluation clear to students. In this case, we have a school which has begun a process which will reap greater rewards each year it continues to work on clarifying the rubrics and scoring criteria which accompany their performance assessments. In and of itself, this is a vast improvement in our efforts to know better what our students truly know and are able to do — and it serves them better in achieving outcomes of significance which will pay dividends in the future.

BRONXVILLE HIGH SCHOOL 9TH GRADE INTERDISCIPLINARY SCORING CRITERIA

Two criteria from Bronxville's High School's interdisciplinary program provide examples to instruct us on improving rubric/criteria development. One is for a "Renaissance Tour" project (fig. 5.4) and the other is a Writing Assessment Criteria (Fig. 5.5). The first was teacher-designed and presented to students, the second was developed *with* the students. As with the other rubrics and scoring criteria presented so far, there are strengths and weaknesses to explore.

RENAISSANCE TOUR — WHAT WORKS

The scoring criteria is consistent in presenting three indicators in each grade category. These present students with a clear guide as to *what* is expected in the project: a map, a written explanation of the map, and an oral presentation of the trip the map represents. The outcomes which the criteria values are clarity, written explanations which are grounded in thoughtful evidence ("why" and "what"), and an ability to think on one's feet in an oral presentation. It is a good starting place, but not without its problems.

WHAT DOESN'T

As with the earlier rubrics, what is meant by "clear," "articulate," or, worse, "fairly clear?" The time taken in #2 under category "A" to explain "logical," for example ("why it makes sense to go from this place to the next, etc."), should be the rule, not the exception. So, while the basic format for the project is articulated in the criteria, the important details which would reflect standards of quality are not presented with enough description. Even though students had done a similar project earlier in the year, there is no mention of that project, no use of it to tease out *exemplars* which might clarify better what levels of quality might be.

IMPLICATIONS

This rubric does show how, even in the absence of benchmarks or exemplary work, teachers can devise rubrics which present stu-

FIGURE 5.4: BRONXVILLE HIGH SCHOOL — RENAISSANCE TOUR SCORING CRITERIA

Criteria: Renaissance Tour

A: 1. A clear, detailed map, precisely showing each place which will be visited during the tour.
2. A well- written explanation of the map which explains WHY each stop was chose & WHAT the historical significance of the stop is. There should be some explanation of why the trip's itinerary is logical — why it makes sense to go from this place to the next, etc.
3. A clear, articulate oral presentation explaining the trip, fielding questions with responsive, articulate answers.

B: 1. A fairly clear, fairly detailed map indicating where the tour will go, but lacking precise details or clarity in parts.
2. A written explanation of the map which explains WHY the stops were chosen but doesn't go into depth about the historical significance of the stop. It briefly explains the logic behind the trip's planning but doesn't connect the stops in a well-explained fashion.
3. A clear, fairly articulate presentation of the trip which answers most questions intelligently and accurately.

C: 1. A map presents the tour, and each place visited, but is not highly detailed or precise. It would not be immediately clear to someone what the purpose of the map was.
2. A written explanation of the tour which tells WHERE each stop is and gives a brief reason as to WHY the stop is being made but lacks any significant historical detail.
3. An oral presentation superficially explains the stops of the tour without elaboration and questions are not fully or clearly answered.

D: 1. A map is drawn with indications of where the tour might stop. Minimal effort has been made; minimal results are shown.
2. A written explanation of the map is equally sketchy and minimal in its effort and results.
3. Oral presentation reveals that the map and writing author have not fully researched the topic and are not in command of the assignment.

E: Work is not turned in by deadline and/or is of such poor quality as to not be recognizable in relation to the assignment given.

FIGURE 5.5: BRONXVILLE HIGH SCHOOL —
WRITING ASSESSMENT CRITERIA

Writing Assessment Criteria

Exemplary/Excellent ("A")

- Good use of accurate details (intelligently selective)
- Interesting - appeals to a wide audience
- Clearly makes its points, doesn't run-on or ramble
- Appropriate vocabularly / Good diction
- Correct mechanics, clear knowledge of mechanics
- Well-organized
- Smooth transitions

Good ("B")

- Appropriate use of details (some lacking)
- Attempts to appeal to a wide audience; style is basically "smooth"
- Clear thesis, makes its points with an occasional run-on
- Vocabulary is adequate; little or no mis-use of words
- Occasional mechanical errors
- Generally well-organized; some problem with transitions

Acceptable ("C")

- Misuse or lack of detail in significant places
- Transitions are weak or missing in places
- Narrow point of view; appeals to a limited audience
- Point may be distinct/clear BUT needs more support or details
- Organized but lacks focus, details (Doesn't clearly follow thesis at times)
- Limited vocabulary
- Mechanical errors.

Unacceptable ("D"/"F")

- Failure to use details or facts effectively
- Rambles, runs-on
- Poorly organized
- Simplistic vocabulary, misused or inappropriate diction
- Numerous mechanical errors
- No clear thesis or point of view

dents with a higher level of clarity. Though it is inconsistent, there are attempts at detailed explanations. Aside from the example presented in *What Doesn't*, #1 in the "C" category attempts to portray imprecision by stating, "It would not be immediately clear to someone what the purpose of the map was." By giving students cues like this, it becomes clearer to them what the expectations for quality work are, and provides them with the questions they need to critique their own work.

GRADE WRITING ASSESSMENT CRITERIA — DEVELOPING A RUBRIC WITH STUDENTS

The most significant feature of this rubric is that it was developed *with the students*. So, flawed though it may be, the students were "present at the creation" and, as a result, had a far better idea of what the rubric's intent was. It's worth taking a moment here to describe the process behind this rubric's development.

Students were asked to bring in what they believed was an "excellent" piece of writing. There were no restrictions placed on them. They could bring in a *Calvin and Hobbes* cartoon strip, a Sidney Sheldon novel, or *War and Peace* — as long as they could *explain why* they thought it was "excellent." They then were divided into groups of four or five and shared with each other their selections, explaining why they believed their selection was excellent.

From those discussions, students were asked to identify three to five characteristics (indicators) which they had heard people in their group consistently mention in explanation of their selection. Each group posted its list of indicators and from the collected lists, the criteria in Figure 5.5 were determined.

This method is one way to develop rubrics for any variety of skills we want students to pay careful attention to. It announces that we believe these skills to be important — that they count. So, you can ask students to identify great public speakers or "effective listeners" and then get them to focus on the characteristics which make those people excellent at what they do. From those characteristics come lists of indicators which can serve as the baseline for a rubric to score student performance. I was introduced to this method in a workshop with Grant Wiggins, and have found it to be extremely effective on two counts: first, it incorporates the students and thus invests them in it; and second, the indicators serve as a excellent jumping off point for developing more sophisticated and detailed rubrics in the future.

WHAT WORKS

There is a certain amount of attention paid to mechanics and organization, but, interestingly, it also considers *audience*. There is a genuine awareness on the part of the students who helped devise this rubric that *style* is an essential ingredient in good writing — appealing to an audience, being "intelligently selective" in the use of detail, making "smooth transitions," all indicate an awareness of tone which goes beyond "appropriate vocabulary." The consistent focus on clarity, organization, and evidentiary support of points are all solid criteria.

WHAT DOESN'T

Without benchmarks or exemplars — or at least some of the specific examples students may have used in class when devising this criteria — it is, once again, difficult to be sure about what "accurate details" or "interesting" really means. And, once again, the question about quality *has to* be raised. What is the standard to which the writers aspire with this criteria? Is it Sidney Sheldon or Leo Tolstoy? And what determines the difference? So, while this may be a valuable *guideline* for student writing, it still falls short regarding the development of a culture which values high quality writing.

IMPLICATIONS

The inclusion of students in developing this scoring criteria is significant. It opens the door for greater student inclusion and investment in defining what quality work will be and what appropriate standards might look like. This approach encourages students to become active participants in discussions about the teaching/learning process and important contributors in the debates about standards and quality. So, while it still has a long way to go as a scoring criteria, the Writing Assessment Criteria's *process* is a good first step toward developing new ways to assess student work around the issue of quality.

SUMMARY: STANDARDS, CRITERIA, AND RUBRICS

This chapter has provided teachers, students, parents, and administrators with ideas and examples to start a conversation about developing standards. Because students seldom know the expectations for the *quality* of their work, they proceed blindly through school, accepting subjective judgments about their progress. The provocation presented here asks that we open up the conversation about standards to the entire learning community; that teachers be given time to discuss this; and that administrators facilitate the progress of that conversation. This is a challenging task and it takes years to make progress. But consider the stakes: Can we afford to continue as we have, processing students through our classrooms, presenting them with material and tasks, and **not** providing clear feedback against known and valued standards? Is it fair to ask students to "achieve" *without* a clear enunciation of criteria and rubrics to work from?

Arguments can be made about the time and money which might be required to implement such a system of assessment, but those, ultimately, are arguments about priorities. If we do, indeed, care about the quality of student work, if we do, indeed, want our students to make continued *progress* toward standards of high quality, we can use our creativity and ingenuity to achieve those ends. Certainly it is a difficult and challenging task, and mistakes will be made along the way — but will those mistakes be any worse for our students than what they are subjected to now?

Clarifying standards, defining criteria, and developing rubrics is a worthy task for any number of reasons — the most important of which is the progress of our students. If we care about preparing our students for the 21st century, and if we believe performance assessments are an integral part of that preparation, there is little choice in the matter. To develop an performance assessment system *without* these deep and important conversations about standards, criteria, and rubrics would be to miss the point. The shift to new forms of assessment automatically means a shift in school culture, a changing of norms, the developing of new habits of instruction and evaluation. It is, on the face of it, an awesome task. It requires hard, ongoing work on the part of every member of a learning community. It means venturing into new territory, taking risks, changing our work and ourselves. But if the progress and success of our students is, in fact, our central concern, we have little choice in the matter.

We are at a significant point in our history. The standards debate gets to the heart of our visions of schooling in America. In many ways, the United States has become an emerging nation again, with scores of new immigrants, with the drive for inclusion and main-streaming, with the Information Age upon us, we are faced with a set of challenges similar to those of the early 20th century. Despite our military and economic power, our educational system has stag-nated; an outdated framework in a careening age. The greatest experiment in the Great Experiment of Democracy, the public school system, is faced with challenges its 19th century framework cannot meet. The factory system and Industrial Age have passed. The stand-ards debate is one which is taking place in a new age, facing a new century. It demands that we begin the hard conversations about change which will lead to the transformation of our schools. The Great Experiment demands it and the school system requires it. It is incumbent upon us to accept the challenge.

6

TEACHER, TEACH THYSELF: SELF-EDUCATION FOR ASSESSMENT REFORM

Those who began moving into the world of "alternative" assessments in the mid-1980s were at a distinct disadvantage compared to practitioners who begin their search for new assessment methods today. Because this was truly unexplored territory, much of what occurred in the early years of the school restructuring movement was based on theories and "best guesses." In the mid-1990s, we are fortunate, because a steady stream of literature, both theoretical and practical, has been produced since the early 1990s, based on the work of those early pioneers.

Because people have begun to put theory to paper and document the work in the field, today's teacher has the distinct advantage of being able to survey that field to determine what directions she or he may want to go with performance assessments. There are numerous conferences, many sponsored by major professional organizations, and excellent consultants throughout the country available to work with classroom practitioners, administrators, etc. A good place to begin considering what's out there, what might work in your classroom, and what makes sense for a particular situation in a particular school, is to investigate the literature.

To help teachers in that search, this chapter critiques a number of texts which have proven invaluable to many practitioners who embarked on the road to performance assessment. The hope is that these critiques can save teachers some time in their search for those texts which could prove most helpful in their work. While it is *not* an exhaustive list (see the Bibliography for more titles), it reviews those books which I have found most helpful in my own work and in my work consulting with other teachers around the country.

An excellent place to begin one's self-education on performance assessment is Ruth Mitchell's *Testing for Learning: How New Approaches to Evaluation can Improve American Schools.* Published by The Free Press (New York, NY) in 1992, this is an excellent, comprehensive work which blends theory with practical examples, along with a solid dose of the author's own views. Mitchell, who was Associate Director of the Council for Basic Education when this was written, makes it clear in her preface that "The topic here is a new system, not just modified tests" (p. viii). Mitchell helps the reader through the jargon of the new assessments and makes a cogent argument as to why schools need to move away from testing and toward assessment. As was presented earlier in this book, her argument is based on the premise that testing drives curriculum and instruction, and only through assessments which are embedded in curriculum and instruction will we develop a system which promotes authentic teaching and learning.

Mitchell provides a nice mixture of the practical with the theoretical throughout her text. Using examples from statewide systems in California, Arizona, and Maryland, she presents new approaches to assessing writing and follows that with a chapter on performance assessments in Science and Mathematics. These areas are always problematic, particularly on the secondary level, and Mitchell's chapter focuses primarily on 4th and 8th grade examples from California, New York, and Maryland. Her use of the Connecticut Science and Mathematics assessments is particularly useful to secondary teachers, however, and provides a fine explanation of the *process* for developing performance assessments in these fields. Surprisingly, she does not refer to the National Council of Teachers of Mathematics (NCTM) standards and assessments, which have grown to be seen as a benchmark in this area (and are recommended reading for *all* teachers, no matter what discipline). Nonetheless, this is a useful and practical survey for teachers.

To her credit, Ruth Mitchell has written an entire chapter on "Getting Students, Parents, and the Community into the Act." Too often, these constituencies are forgotten players in the assessment drama. Ranging from East Harlem, New York, to Bozeman, Montana, and investigating the Odyssey of the Mind program developed in Calabasas, California, Mitchell notes over and over again the importance of including parents, students, and community members in the development and implementation of performance assessments. This is not a simple public relations or publicity ploy, from Mitchell's point of view, but an essential element in the intelligent and effective implementation of those assessments which can improve the educational system. Her advice is wise, thoughtful, and necessary.

The most useful chapter, and probably the most "used" chapter in *Testing for Learning* is the one on portfolios. With extensive examples from the field, Mitchell presents a cogent argument for the practicality and usefulness of portfolio assessment — and provides numerous jumping-off points for those interested! Presenting a wide variety of examples from around the country, this chapter is essential reading for anyone considering implementing a portfolio system.

The remainder of the book investigates the history of testing, and how America became caught in the "testing trap," as well as the problems raised by performance assessments — particularly in developing reliability in rating and clarity in vocabulary. She presents her ideas for "next steps," and even though the book was published in 1992, many of the issues are still current (the cost of performance assessment relative to wide-scale standardized testing, are these tests fair to all students, and so on). In all, this is an excellent book to start one's investigation of the breadth of performance assessments which are possible, providing solid theoretical grounding with fine practical examples.

Two of the earliest and most thoughtful pioneers in the performance assessment movement were Richard Stiggins and Grant Wiggins (is there some connection between an " — iggins" surname and one's inclination to study performance assessment?). In late 1993 and early 1994, each came out with a book based on their years of work. Grant Wiggins's *Assessing Student Performance: Exploring the Purpose and Limits of Testing* (Jossey-Bass, 1993) is, at heart, a philosophical and theoretical work but, because Wiggins is out working with teachers in schools all over the country, it has an important practical side to it. Richard Stiggins's **Student-Centered Classroom Assessment** (Merrill, 1994) is in a textbook format and should be required reading in **all** teacher education programs in this country, as well as present in every faculty room and at every in-service day in schools. Together, with Mitchell's book, these works can provide a classroom teacher with a solid foundation in both the theory and practice of performance assessment.

Grant Wiggins makes no apology that his book is philosophical in nature. "Philosophy brings unthinking habits to the surface; it clarifies conceptual confusion in common practices and talk. And there are just too many unexamined habits and confused ideas about testing, whether we look at nationally given tests or teacher-designed tests" (p. xii). So, while portions of the book consider the *morality* of testing, much of it is very practical philosophy (if that's not an oxymoron) because it provokes the reader to seriously consider **all** the facets and implications of assessment systems.

Because his initial work with the Coalition of Essential Schools and his present endeavors as the director of the Center for Learning, Assessment, and School Structure (C.L.A.S.S.) has always taken Wiggins *into the field*, his consideration of assessment practice is always useful. A brilliant thinker, Wiggins is not some navel-gazing philosopher contemplating "the best of all possible worlds." He constantly pushes himself and those he works with to probe more deeply, to look at student work carefully, reflectively, and with an eye to better inform the teacher and student as to how well assessments are working. So, while *Assessing Student Performance* presents a thorough history (refutation) of the testing system we now have, as well as a deeply thoughtful philosophical argument for changing assessments, it is also filled with authentic and practical examples of how teachers *are* changing assessment practice in the schools. It is significant, I think, to include this book as a "must read" for teachers working on changing their assessment, because too often educational reform has been undermined by simplistic "how to" books which are ungrounded in a thoughtful, intelligent philosophy. In Grant Wiggins, we have a first-rate intellectual who has applied his thinking to the important foundational questions surrounding testing and assessment. If we hope to move the assessment system in this country, Wiggins's book provides an essential component because it clearly answers the "why change?" question in a practical, yet philosophical manner.

Richard Stiggins's first chapter in **Student-Centered Classroom Assessment**, "A Principled View of Classroom Assessment," echoes many of Wiggins's philosophical tenets, but make no mistake — this is a textbook for change. Significantly, Stiggins frames the creation of new assessments in a "both/and" context with standardized and teacher-created testing, avoiding the pitfall of the "either/or" argument. In all, this is a very practical, though huge (441 pages), text. Stiggins has divided his 16 chapters into four sections: "Understanding the Classroom Assessment Context" (Chapters 1–5), "Understanding Assessment Methods" (Chapters 6–9), "Classroom Applications" (Chapters 10–13), and "Communicating About Student Achievement" (Chapters 14–16). Each chapter sets out "Objectives" at the beginning and concludes with a summary and "exercises to advance your learning." Clearly, the view of teacher (or future teacher) as learner is intended.

It would be a mistake for the classroom practitioner to skip to the "applications" section of this book without examining the first two parts of the text. Stiggins has worked long and thoughtfully in this field and the framework he constructs in parts one and two are essential to understanding not only the *how*, but also the **why**, of part three on "applications." He tackles the hard questions, offers reasoned answers, and presents hundreds of practical suggestions, templates, and forms in the course of the book. There are parts of this book which might be skimmed in its initial reading but the reader will surely go back to those sections as she or he begins to implement performance assessments.

An important component of *Student-Centered Classroom Assessment*, is the time and consideration Stiggins gives to matters like national standardized tests and report card grading. With a clear eye on the realities of the present system's "coin of the realm," Stiggins offers a number of innovative and practical suggestions, as well as thoughtful provocations for moving into new territory regarding both testing and reporting student progress. This is a useful and significant book and, with Mitchell's and Wiggins's, provides the novice assessment innovator with a solid foundation in both theory and practice.

The Association for Supervision and Curriculum Development (ASCD) has been prominent in the development and dissemination of new ideas in teaching since the end of World War II. In the past decade, it has distinguished itself through its monthly publication, *Educational Leadership*, and its practical publications for teachers and administrators. While membership dues are a bit steep (around $75.00 per year), most teachers can find copies of *Educational Leadership* in their staff development center or by asking administrators if they subscribe. It is well worth the effort. The monthly magazine consistently presents well-written articles about cutting-edge practices and debates, and the periodic publication (several of which are described below) allows teachers to probe new concepts in greater depth.

Starting in 1991, ASCD began publishing *at least* one book a year on new assessment techniques. These books are particularly useful to teachers for a number of reasons. First, they generally present the best thinking about current practice available at the time of publication. Second, they are relatively short (usually between 60 and 150 pages), making them accessible to time-burdened practitioners. Third, they are often edited collections of work or organized in a fashion that allows sections to be read and reflected upon without disrupting the day-to-day work of teachers. Significantly, the consistent publication from year-to-year serves to update previous ideas and practices, building a sense of development for the reader. Finally, the books are very practical — exactly the kind a classroom teacher can sink his or her teeth into and find informative and useful.

In 1991, ASCD published *Expanding Student Assessment*, a book of collected essays edited by Vito Perrone, Dean of the Harvard

Graduate School of Education. The 10 essays presented span everything from standards to documentation and consider performance assessment applications in a variety of subject areas. In clearly-written and well-reasoned essays by professors, researchers, and even a 6th grade teacher, this volume provides today's teacher with an historical view of "alternative" assessment, while providing some practical and philosophical insights into this reform movement. Much of what is found here reinforces the foundational works of Mitchell, Wiggins, and Stiggins, while providing some new lenses to view those ideas through.

In 1992, *A Practical Guide to Performance Assessment*, written by Joan L. Herman, Pamela R. Aschbacher, and Lynn Winters, three California-based researchers, was published. Classroom teachers are generally suspicious of researchers, and there is a general attitude "in the field" that the research community doesn't really understand the complexities of what goes on in classroom. This book puts that argument to rest. The title, in fact, is quite appropriate — this *is* a very practical guide for those considering new assessment practices. In a systematic and easily understood text, the authors present a logical and useful process for moving into the implementation of performance assessments. As with many ASCD books, there are numerous charts, graphs, and "bulleted" lists which enhance the understanding of the concepts presented in the text. In the same fashion, there are some very practical templates provided for consideration, particularly in the area of scoring rubrics. As noted above, this publication is a developmental giant step from *Expanding Student Assessment*, providing some very practical "how's" to implement that book's "why's."

Later in 1992, Ronald Brandt, the director of ASCD, edited a collection of readings from *Educational Leadership* and published *Performance Assessment.* This compilation, which includes essays from 1987 through 1992, provides the reader with some of the most interesting and thoughtful work from teachers, researchers, and professors *as it was happening*. So, while much of this work still reads as imaginative and fresh, it is also a wonderful historical document of the development of the performance assessment movement. Many of the most prominent thinkers in the assessment field are represented here. Along with Grant Wiggins, members of Harvard's Project Zero group, Howard Gardner and Dennie Palmer Wolf, as well as Lorrie Shepard, George Madaus, Rex Brown, Joan Boykoff Baron, and Richard Shavelson appear in the volume. Beyond the "big names" there are lesser known, but no less thoughtful, authors whose work can help any teacher who aspires to implement performance assessments. Divided into five sections, the volume considers "The Need for Change," "Portfolios," "Assessment in Early Childhood," "Performance Assessment," and "Tying Assessments to Standards, Curriculum, and Desired Student Outcomes." Because it is a collection of essays, this is an easy book to pick up, read an essay, and put down, reflecting on what one has read. It is well-organized and incredibly useful.

In 1993, ASCD turned to two organizations prominent in the development of new assessments for publications. *Graduation by Exhibition: Assessing Genuine Achievement* features the work of members of the Coalition of Essential Schools and *Assessing Student Outcomes* originated in Colorado's McREL Institute. Both these groups have been working on the development and implementation of performance assessments since the beginning of the school restructuring movement and each book has value in its own way.

Graduation by Exhibition was organized by the Coalition's Senior Researcher, Joseph P. McDonald, and features the work of three high schools in their efforts to implement Graduation-by-Exhibition systems. In essays written by a school principal and three teachers, this book provides the reader with an insider's look at the ups and downs of performance assessment implementation. Most importantly, these are *true* stories from schools in the midst of implementation and change. The authenticity and candidness of the authors' voices (Sidney Smith, Dorothy Turner, Marain Finney, and Eileen Barton) will strike a responsive chord in any classroom practitioner. The value of this book is that it presents a "warts-and-all" account of the difficulties and complexities of assessment implementation in a very direct and honest fashion.

Assessing Student Outcomes: Performance Assessment Using the Dimensions of Learning Model is based on the work of Robert Marzano and his colleagues and coauthors, Debra Pickering and Jay McTighe. Marzano has developed a framework for considering the acquisition and application of knowledge, the Dimensions of Learning Model. This model's elements are: *Positive Attitudes and Perceptions about Learning; Acquiring and Integrating Knowledge; Extend-*

ing and Refining Knowledge; Using Knowledge Meaningfully; and *Productive Habits of Mind.* ASCD had published a detailed account of Marzano's Dimensions of Learning in a earlier publication, but this book zeroes in on the *application of the system.* While philosophically grounded, this text presents a number of practical ideas and examples which classroom teachers will undoubtedly find useful. At the very least, Marzano, Pickering, and McTighe's book will provoke thought, leading teachers to reconsider *why* they do *what* they do *the way* they do! So, while not necessarily a "must read" text, classroom practitioners would do well to find this book and consider its applications to their setting.

Another organization involved in teacher training and publications is IRI/Skylight Publishing, Palantine, Illinois. Originally started as the Illinois Renewal Institute, the demand for teacher training in new methods and an alliance with Phi Delta Kappan led to the rapid growth of this organization nationally. They are now the International Renewal Institute and have a national staff of teacher trainers who work in areas ranging from authentic assessment to ungraded schools to applying Howard Gardner's "Multiple Intelligences" theory to classroom practice. They publish widely, and many of their books are "how to" types, with numerous charts, graphs, templates, and forms for teachers to use. In relation to that, I would urge a word of caution: the IRI/Skylight books can be extremely useful when used *in conjunction with* some kind of ongoing teacher-training program, whether IRI's or not. To simply buy one of these books off the shelf and begin using it in the classroom could lead to the worst kind of perversion of the intent. That said, let's look at two of IRI/Skylight books which can be extremely useful to teachers.

Kay Burke is now vice president of instructional services for IRI/Skylight, but started as a classroom teacher and administrator, and knows schools well enough to have edited a fine book — *Authentic Assessment: A Collection* (1992) — and written another — *The Mindful School: How to Assess Thoughtful Outcomes* (1993). The *Collection* book is similar to ASCD's and we see a number of familiar names reappear: Grant Wiggins, Lorrie Shepard, Rex Brown, and George Madaus are all in this compilation. There is even a little overlap with those authors. No matter, this is a well-organized and fine collection. Broken into five sections — *Assessing Assessment,*

Testing and Thoughtfulness, Alternatives to Testing, Journals and Port-folios, and *Significant Outcomes* — this is a nice parallel collection to use with the ASCD anthology. Pieces by Art Costa, Fred Newman, and Jay McTighe (with Steven Ferrara) are all outstanding pieces and this collection also includes Rick Stiggins's wonderful essay "Assessment Literacy," which originally appeared in *Phi Delta Kappan* (March, 1991). In all, this is a collection which any teacher interested in deepening his or her knowledge of performance assessment practice should become familiar with.

How to Assess Thoughtful Outcomes is part of IRI/Skylight's "The Mindful School" series and is formatted like a workbook, replete with charts and templates which are ready for use. It is a straightforward and clear book, extremely user-friendly, and touches all the important bases. Starting with a chapter on "Thoughtful Outcomes," Burke makes her case about the limits of standardized testing and the problems with teacher-made tests in early chapters, before getting to the nitty-gritty of performance assessments. Her chapters on "Portfolios" and "Performances and Exhibitions" are full of sound, practical advice, with very useful examples and process tips throughout. Likewise, the penultimate chapter on "Interviews and Conferences." The middle section of the book — "Projects," "Learning Logs and Journals," "Metacognitive Reflection," "Observation Checklists," and "Graphic Organizers" — present methods in a rather formulaic fashion and a major concern is that teachers could easily adapt these methods without **thinking about changing their practice**. The danger of a workbook format, in fact, is that too many teachers, pressured by time and administrators who want to see "change," will simply *substitute* some of the templates or chart for what they already do, without ever seriously rethinking their views about assessment. Nonetheless, *How to Assess Thought-ful Outcomes* is an extremely useful book for those teachers who are genuinely reconsidering their classroom work and want to be presented with examples of "how to" do it.

The National Center for Fair and Open Testing (FairTest) sits in a big white house on the corner of Broadway and Inman St. in Cambridge, Massachusetts. If Ralph Nader had ever focused on reforming the testing practices in this country, he would have started FairTest. This organization relentlessly battled the Educational Testing Service (ETS), the College Board, and a host of other testing companies before alternative testing became popularized in this new wave of educational reform. With new ammunition, however, FairTest has not only increased its pressure on those organizations but has also produced some of the finest publications to combat standardized testing as well as inform teachers and parents about performance assessments.

Two short publications from FairTest, *Implementing Performance Assessments: A Guide to Classroom, School, and System Reform* and *Standardized Tests and Our Children: A Guide to Testing Reform*, are comprehensive, crystal clear presentations delineating the ills of standardization and the practical possibilities of performance assessments.

In *Implementing Performance Assessments*, FairTest's authors (Monty Neill, Phyllis Bursh, Bob Schaeffer, Carolyn Thall, Marilyn Yohe, and Pamela Zappardino) move the reader through the arguments against traditional testing, possibilities for alternatives, and, most significantly, carefully examining classroom evaluation and scoring as well as validity questions. They also spend time considering what is required to create schoolwide change — a nice primer for the individual teacher who might be looking ahead to bringing others into this process.

Implementing Performance Assessments covers much of the ground other books listed have — and, again, there is some liberal cross-referencing (you'll find Kay Burke and Dennie Palmer Wolf directly cited, for example) but the sections on *validity* and *accountability* are particularly notable because few of the other books touch on these topics as this one does. Since new assessments will be compared to standardized measures, whether we think they should or not, we need to be able to understand the language psychometricians (testmakers) use and effectively counter their arguments. At the very least, performance assessments should address the questions of validity, generalizability, reliability, and accountability. While by no means exhaustive, FairTest's handling of these topics in this book are an excellent place to start. Forewarned is forearmed, as it were, and the novice assessment designer should be cognizant of the arguments about validity and accountability which are being debated. With brief but clear explanations, *Implementing Performance Assessments* performs an important service to that end, equipping even the novice designer with the basic information which needs to be considered when assessing the assessments.

Standardized Tests and Our Children: A Guide to Testing Reform should be read by *everyone,* regardless of one's views about performance assessments and standardized testing. Once again, FairTest concisely presents the problems and dilemmas schools are faced with because of the tyranny of standardized measurement of students. By carefully examining *how* standardized tests are used, looking at the history of testing in this country, and detailing how these tests work, FairTest provides a solid foundation which more than adequately prepares anyone to debate the use of these tests. In the section entitled "What's wrong with standardized tests?," a body of compelling examples provide important information any teacher, parent, administrator, or student should know about these examinations. Because FairTest is an activist organization, they once again include a "What you can do" section along with a list of resources and readings which cite a number of the sources presented in this chapter, along with others.

FairTest's campaign for better assessment is ongoing. This is a valuable organization to be aware of, providing resources and support for the performance assessment movement. For any teacher embarking down the road of new assessments, the clear and concise materials available from FairTest are a valuable resource, offering support and guidance in this new territory.

David Perkins is codirector of Harvard's Project Zero, the research center for cognitive development, and has contributed a number of thoughtful articles to *Educational Leadership* which examine why and how performance assessments should be used. His book, *Smart Schools: From Training Memories to Educating Minds* (The Free Press, New York, NY, 1992), is a provocative and carefully reasoned study about why schools, as they are presently structured, are not teaching young people to use their minds well. Drawing from work by Theodore Sizer and Mortimer Adler, Perkins adds his own substantial contribution to the vision of how schools could operate more effectively. His chapter on "Teaching and Learning" is particularly useful to classroom teachers engaged in change. Beyond that, his consideration of curriculum, content, and motivation are all sections which will provoke *any* teacher (or student, or parent, or administrator) to reconsider how school is constituted versus with how it might be viewed. This is an easily-read book, formatted in a fashion that logically builds the reader's momentum while offering some wonderful practical examples of how classrooms might change *right now*. Because Perkins is ultimately interested in cognitive development and the performance of higher-order critical thinking skills by students, this is a particularly useful book for teachers to read. So much of today's curriculum and instruction is mired in lower-order thinking skills (the "Training Memories" part of Perkins's title) that teachers often don't push themselves to think about what a school where students exhibited higher-order thinking skills might look like. *Smart Schools* provides us with a text that pushes our imaginations while offering practical possibilities and is a highly recommended addition to one's assessment library.

The most problematic areas for performance assessments are mathematics and science. Because of the breadth of content and the assumption that there is a "right way" to teach these subjects, change has occurred slowly in these disciplines, despite the NCTM standards and now the Science benchmarks. For teachers in these areas with a desire to consider change, I would point to the work of Gerald Kulm and the three books he has produced since 1990, along with Joan Countryman's *Writing in Mathematics* as excellent initial readings. Kulm's edited books, *Assessing Higher Order Thinking in Mathematics* and *Science Assessment in the Service of Reform* (both American Association for the Advancement of Science Publications), and his recent *Mathematics Assessment: What Works in the Classroom* (Jossey-Bass, 1994), are all thought-provoking and practical — in short, useful.

The two books Kulm has edited are collections of essays written by researchers and discipline-based professors. As mentioned earlier, classroom practitioners are often leery of work which comes from the university or the research labs. In this case, however, it is well worth a look at what has been generated from these authors. Starting with a view of "current perspectives" the books consider changes which have occurred in mathematics and science thinking in the last decade and how that potentially impacts the work of classroom teachers. The idea of looking for a continuum of student progress in problem-solving or concept-development, for example, would necessarily move teachers away from the traditional "auditing" of student work: "Is Johnny 'keeping up' with us? No. Well, we have to move on anyway." What is clear in this new perspective is that curriculum, instruction, and assessment are integrally interwoven. It is not enough to simply "move on" to the next chapter if we do not consider the progress (or lack of progress) our students are achieving.

Kulm and the various authors are extremely aware of the impact of technology on the fields of science and mathematics and spend considerable time addressing that concern. It is not unconnected to the focus the books place on the idea of research and development, too. In all, what these books are pointing to is *an entirely new approach* to the way mathematics and science **are perceived** as part of the curriculum. As discussed throughout this book, once we move into considering new forms of assessment, all the old rules are thrown out. Because performance assessments *demand* reconsideration of curriculum and instruction, the entire view of *what, how,* and *why* we teach what we do comes into question. The essays in *Assessing Higher Order Thinking in Mathematics* and *Science Assessment in the Service of Reform* bring these points home again and again, demanding a total reconsideration of curriculum, instruction, and assessment in these fields.

Mathematics Assessment: What Works in the Classroom should be read by *any* teacher considering the use of performance assessments. Kulm has provided a much-needed service in publishing this book, and it is a rich and practical volume. The book's organization clearly frames its purpose. Part One is "Background and Perspectives" and reviews, once again, *why* performance assessments need to be considered. Kulm pushes the argument a bit further, however, because he knows his audience. Therefore, a chapter on "Procedural and Conceptual Knowledge," as well as one on "Problem Solving and Strategic Knowledge" are both included in the "Backgrounds and Perspectives" section. In doing this, Kulm not only recognizes the particular differences mathematicians deal with in their field, but speaks to that audience "in their own language." To his credit, the writing is clear and straightforward and any nonmathematician may both understand what Kulm is discussing, and also extrapolate from the discussion how the concepts might apply to new assessments in other disciplines.

Part Two, "Planning and Designing an Assessment Program," might well be retitled as "A Common-Sense Approach to Developing

New Assessments." Kulm provides the reader with an intelligent, rational process which clearly delineates *how* to get started, *what* to look for, and *how to* begin to change classroom practice. With chapters focusing on "Individual Mathematical Performance," "Group Mathematical Performance," "Student Self-Assessment and Affective Factors," and "Scoring and Grading Techniques," Kulm covers all the important bases both philosophically and practically.

The third section of *Mathematics Assessment* is about "Classroom Assessment Models," and Kulm distinguishes himself again by providing the reader with *real* work from *real* teachers. Divided into chapters which investigate Elementary, Middle, and High Schools, as well as a commentary on "Effects of Performance Assessments in Mathematics Classrooms," teachers involved in creating new assessments would do well to read this *entire* section carefully. It was stated earlier that teachers from *any* discipline would profit from reading this book about mathematics. In the same fashion, teachers from any level — primary, middle, or secondary — can *learn* from reading about the assessment approaches and actual examples described in Part Three. Because performance assessments is such new territory, it reopens the possibilities for teachers across disciplines and grade levels to begin new and exciting dialogue about teaching and learning. Gerald Kulm has thrown that door wide open with this excellent book on mathematics assessment.

When thinking about publications which might advance our thinking on creating new forms of assessment for our students, it is probably unlikely that one would consider the United States Government as an important source. Wrong! Two publications, one from the executive branch and one from the legislative branch, in fact, have a great deal to offer teachers in their consideration of new assessments. At the very least, these publications offer strong support for moving into new directions in assessing student work.

In June 1991, the U.S. Department of Labor published the SCANS report for America 2000: *What Work Requires of Schools*. SCANS is an acronym for The Secretary's Commission on Achieving Necessary Skills. The secretary, in this case, was Secretary of Labor Lynn Martin of George Bush's administration. The SCANS study group was comprised of business, labor, social service, and education leaders from across the country. Companies like Aetna Insurance,

IBM, GTE, MCI Communications, and RJR Nabisco were represented, as were the AFL/CIO and the UAW. The 30-member commission reads as an impressive coalition of the business, labor, service, and educational communities. I bring this up, as well as the fact that this commission worked under the auspices of the Bush Administration — certainly no hotbed of "radical" political or social leanings — because the findings and recommendations have important implications for teachers.

While the SCANS report is focused primarily on making sure the United States has a "world-class" economy throughout the 21st century, it perceives of the schools as a place where students will need to learn the skills necessary to provide a "world-class" workforce. Whether one philosophically agrees with this notion (are schools simply prevocational training institutions?) or not, is not the issue for us here. What the commission *says* about schools is significant. Creating a simple analogy: "Traditional (workplace) Model: High Performance Model = Schools of Today: Schools of Tomorrow," the finding are encouraging for anyone interested in moving into new assessments.

According to the SCANS report, in "Schools of Tomorrow":

◆ (The) focus (will be) on development of thinking skills.

◆ Assessment (will be) integral to teaching.

◆ Students (will) actively construct knowledge for themselves.

◆ (The schools will be) learner-centered, teacher directed.

◆ Skills (will be) learned in context of real problems.

The list certainly sounds like guidelines for a performance assessment system. The conclusions of the SCANS group, in fact, match the basic philosophical tenets of the school reform movement. As they see it, every fundamental aspect of how schools are organized and run needs to be reconsidered in light of a world which has undergone unprecedented and unforeseen technological, social, and political change. This is not a group of "radical" teachers or reformers calling for these changes. If we need to look for support for the ideas and concepts behind the creation of a new assessment system we need go no further than the SCANS report.

The Office of Technology Assessment, an arm of the United States Congress, has compiled what is possibly the most comprehensive examination of the history of testing in this country and others, with a clear eye toward the changes in testing technological advances are bringing, in its February, 1992, publication *Testing in American Schools: Asking the Right Questions*. Hundreds of people contributed to the creation of this 300-page, large format book, and many familiar names appear: George Madaus, Ruth Mitchell, Joan Boykoff Baron, FairTest, Howard Gardner, Theodore Sizer, Grant Wiggins, and Dennie Palmer Wolf, to name a few. Again, it is telling to note that, as with the SCANS report, performance assessment reform is no longer seen as "outside" or "beyond" the mainstream. In the case of *Testing in American Schools*, almost 20% of the book is devoted to "Performance Assessments: Methods and Characteristics." Considering that other sections include Future Technologies and "Testing in Transition," it becomes clear that this is the Congress's version, in its own particular frame, of the SCANS report. While this is not an "essential read" for teachers who are moving into performance assessments, this book can serve as an extremely valuable reference work. It is the type of text one can pick up, read a portion of, and put down — leaving with some valuable new information in the process. At the very least, those becoming involved in new assessments should know that works like *Testing in America* and the *SCANS Report* are out there to be read and referred to.

Several other books to consider investigating when initially researching new assessment practices are *Student Engagement and Achievement in American Secondary Schools* (Fred M. Newmann, ed; Teachers College Press, New York, NY, 1992), *Toward a New Science of Educational Testing and Assessment* (Berlak, Newman, Adams, Archbald, Burgess, Raven, and Romburg; State University of New York Press, 1992), and *Authentic Assessment in Action* (Darling-Hammond, Ancess, and Falk; Teachers College Press, New York, NY, 1995). Within these covers one will find essays and discussions about new assessment practices across the disciplines, as well as case studies of schools engaged in changing their practice. Rather than summarizing each, I will leave it to the reader to browse these selections and choose what might be most useful. The books reinforce much of what the earlier ones have presented, yet each brings it own distinct perspective to the discourse. They are rich in content and examples, are well written, and contribute to the overall composition of the *what, why,* and *how* of performance assessments.

As was mentioned at the beginning of this chapter, the purpose for critiquing a body of works on new assessments was a simple one: to save people time and leg-work. Since no comprehensive, annotated bibliography of performance assessment texts exists, the hope here is that these reviews can help direct teachers to those sources which might prove most useful. You may discover, after tracking down and reading one of the books mentioned, that it wasn't what you expected, or it didn't quite live up to its critique here. Share that information. Share it with colleagues — who may also read it and agree or disagree with you — and share it with me (a letter to the publisher will reach me). What's important about all of this work is that a *continuing dialogue* exists. This is always *under construction.* As with any new field, the rules shift as we learn more. But if we do not engage in productive, critical discourse with each other, the ideas will die on the vine. So, you are encouraged to question, to challenge, to *engage.* Which leads to some final words about assessment reform and teaching practice.

WHERE WE STAND; WHERE WE MIGHT MOVE

Historically, teaching has been an isolated profession. Individuals do their work in their classrooms with little collegial interaction with their peers. Even though this volume is addressed to those individuals who have begun or will begin the change process in their classrooms, the hope is that they will soon be engaged in the ongoing conversation which is at the heart of genuine school reform. To that end, it is important to address several issues about teaching and change.

One of the greatest problems we face as teachers is our isolation from our colleagues. Too often we work in schools where we not only *never* get to see our colleagues work, but our time is so absorbed in teaching five-a-day (plus "duties") that there isn't any time to ever have a conversation of substance with other teachers. This not only stunts our growth as professionals, but it impoverishes the quality of our work as they years wear on. I don't know anyone who entered the teaching profession hoping to become a "burnout."

Yet we are faced with the problem in every school. In-service courses on "Stress Management" are offered on a regular basis. While genuine collegiality might not be the sole remedy for these problems, it would certainly benefit the adults in school if they were given some quality, professional time together.

Rob Evans, an educational psychologist in the Boston area who has published in *Educational Leadership* and runs workshops for teachers and administrators has pointed out that what most teachers and schools refer to as "collegiality" is, in fact, "congeniality." I think the distinction is important and reflective of the sad state of affairs regarding teacher-to-teacher interaction in most schools. In much the same way, in many schools I have visited the term "professional" or "professionalism" means, "I'm a professional and Bob's a professional — therefore I have no business walking into his classroom and giving him critical feedback about his work." Imagine if doctors acted this way! Picture two surgeons in the Operating Room standing over a patient. One doctor reaches for the wrong instrument during the surgical procedure. Would the other doctor think, "Well, Bob's a professional, and *I'm* a professional, therefore I shouldn't tell him he's going to harm this patient"? The example is ludicrous, of course, but it points to the fact that consulting with colleagues, receiving critical (not negative!) feedback, and developing a relationship based on the *best interest of the client* is **not** part of the teaching profession — yet.

With all the discussion about school reform and school restructuring, there has been little talk about restructuring the *professional stature* of teachers. It is incumbent upon teacher unions to transform themselves as the schools change; to lead their membership *away* from a labor union identification and *toward* professional organization status. One key element in this shift would be support of the National Board of Professional Teaching Standards. This movement, while in process for almost a decade, has just begun certifying teachers. As with Board-certified doctors, lawyers, architects, and accountants, the professionals involved in the job in question certify their incoming members. Think about it. Who certifies teachers and what are the standards for certification? Usually it is the amorphous "State" which certifies and the qualifications for certification are the number of hours completed in certain courses. While this discussion may seem far afield from performance assessment initially, think further. What are the **performance** standards for the teaching profession? Apparently "seat time" is the only qualification necessary.

This is not an easy subject to tackle, but it is a conversation which *must* begin. Moving into new assessments, which requires new methods of instruction and new perspectives on curriculum, the larger can of worms which is school structure is opened. The individual teacher who embarks down this path should anticipate the questions which will be raised, the problems which will arise, the controversies which lurk around every corner.

These ideas are not offered to scare people off. They are simply the realities of the situation. Creating new assessments shifts all the old paradigms and questions all the old assumptions — turning quite a few on their ears. To not be forewarned is to be set-up for failure.

Keep in mind that none of this has to be cast in an "either/or" context and that one key to implementing change is to get people to adopt a problemsolving mode of behavior when faced with new ideas. Rather than drawing lines in the sand — "I'm for/against performance assessments" — a healthy dialogue about *which* assessments and *why* could yield more positive results, while creating better and more engaging work for students. Too often, in schools, we are painted into "either/or" corners — heterogeneous **or** homogeneous grouping; block scheduling **or** the eight-period day; performance assessments **or** standardized tests. The possibilities for "both/and" do not exist if we allow every issue to be cast as a black **or** white decision.

To deal with any of these issues, however, teachers need time. They need time together, as true professionals — the way doctors, lawyers, architects consult with others in their profession. Teachers need to know *what their colleagues do*. It is no longer good enough to simply say, "Sure, I know Keith. He teaches math." Well, *what* does he really teach (algebra, geometry, etc.) and, more significantly, *how* does he teach it? Equally important: *how* does he assess student work? Teachers seldom have the time to have these basic conversations and, as bad, they are not encouraged to.

Despite all these potential controversies, I encourage the individual to begin working with new assessments. It will provoke new conversations, it will enliven your classroom, it will give students — and maybe some colleagues — a new voice. It will generate new

ideas and the exhilarating ups and downs of skydiving. And, sometimes, it will be lonely. And, sometimes, you will bear the brunt
of criticism. Ultimately, I think, you have to weigh all of this against
one question: What's best for the kids? If you sincerely believe that
new assessments will help your students achieve more, that they
will better reveal *how* your students are smart, that they will engage
and energize your classroom with active and curious young people
— then do it! If you have doubts, let me refer you to something
Dennis Gray shared with us when we were doing Socratic Seminar
training with him.

If you don't want to change, there's always a (good?) reason.

1. We tried that before.
2. Our school is different.
3. We don't want to be different.
4. It costs too much.
5. That's not my responsibility.
6. We don't have the time.
7. We don't have enough help.
8. Our school is too small (too large) for it.
9. The union will scream.
10. We've never done it before.
11. It's against district (state) policy.
12. We don't have the authority.
13. That's too ivory tower.
14. Let's get back to reality.
15. That's not our problem.
16. Why change it; it's still working O.K.
17. I don't like the idea.
18. You're right, but . . .
19. You're 2 years ahead of your time.
20. We're not ready for that.
21. We don't have the money, equipment, room, or staff.
22. It isn't in the budget.
23. Good thought, but impractical.
24. Let's give it more thought.
25. Let's put it in writing.
26. Not that again.

27. Where did you dig that one up?
28. We did all right without it.
29. Let's form a committee.
30. Has anyone else ever tried it?
31. I don't see the connection.
32. Maybe that will work in your situation, but not in mine.
33. The Board will never go for it.
34. It's too much trouble to change.
35. I know a fellow who tried it, and it didn't work.
36. It's impossible.
37. We've always done it this way.
38. We're doing it already.

The list is not exhaustive, and I'd encourage people to add to it. The point is, a reason for **not** changing can always be found. What I would like to call for is a Moratorium on "the list." That is, if anyone in your school raises one of the items on the list, the response is, "Sorry, there's a moratorium on that 'reason.' We have to proceed."

As a final note, I will cite Michael Fullan's advice for implementing change: "Ready, fire, aim." All the "pieces" will never be *perfectly* in place; everything will not be aligned "just so." At some point, if you have made a commitment to try new assessments, **do it**. It's just like skydiving. Once you're up in the plane with the parachute on, you might as well jump.

If you've reached this point in the book, you're ready to get into the plane and take off. You've been given the fundamentals, you've met some veterans who have jumped (and who continue to), and you're mulling over whether you've really made the commitment to designing new assessments. The plane's warmed up and ready to go, you've done your preparation. The decision is yours. The last questions I'll leave you with are these: If you **don't** do it, will you look back and see a lost opportunity? Will there be a twinge of regret that you could have taken the risk, that it doesn't look so bad in retrospect? The last thought I'll leave you with is this: Picture your students sitting in your classroom. Knowing what you now know about performance assessments, what would they tell you to do?

BIBLIOGRAPHY

Adler, Mortimer J. (1982) *The Paideia Proposal*, Macmillan Publishing, New York, NY

Adler, Mortimer J. (1983) *Paideia Problems and Possibilities*, Macmillan Publishing, New York, NY

Adler, Mortimer J. (1984) *The Paideia Program*, Macmillan Publishing, New York, NY

Angelo, T. & Cross, K.P. (1993) *Classroom Assessment Techniques*, Jossey-Bass Publishers, San Francisco, CA

Archbald, D. & Newman, F. (1988) *Beyond Standardized Testing: Authentic Academic Achievement in the Secondary School.* Reston, VA: NASSP Publications

Belanoff, P. & Dickson, M. (eds.) (1991) *Portfolios: Process and Product*, Boynton/Cook Publishers, Heinemann, Portsmouth, NH

Berlak, Harold, et al (1992) *Toward a New Science of Educational Testing and Assessment*, NY: State University of New York Press

Board of Education, City of Chicago. (1991) *Introducing the Socratic Seminar into the Secondary School Classroom*, Bd. of Ed. City of Chicago, IL

Brandt, Ronald (ed.) (1992) *Performance Assessment*, ASCD, Alexandria, VA

Burke, Kay (ed.) (1992) *Authentic Assessment: A Collection*, IRI/Skylight Publishing, Palatine, IL

Burke, Kay (1993) *The Mindful School: How to Assess Thoughtful Outcomes*, IRI/Skylight Publishing, Palatine, IL

Edgerton, R., Hutchings, P., & Quinlan, K. (1991) *The Teaching Portfolio*, American Association for Higher Education, Washington, DC

Fairtest, (1990) *Standardized Tests and Out Children: A Guide to Testing Reform*, The National Center for Fair & Open Testing, Cambridge, MA

Fullan, M. (with Stiegelbauer, S.), (1991) *The New Meaning of Educational Change*, Teachers College Press, New York, NY

Gardner, H. (1985) *Frames of Mind*, Basic Books, Inc. Publishers, New York, NY

Graves, D. & Sunstein, B. (eds.) (1992) *Portfolio Portraits*, Heinemann, Portsmouth, NH

Hargreaves, Andy, (1989) *Curriculum and Assessment Reform*, Open University Press, Philadelphia, PA

Harvard Educational Review, (Spring, 1994) *Symposium: Equity in Educational Assessment*, Cambridge, MA

Herman, J., Aschbacher, P. & Winters, L. (1992) *A Practical Guide to Performance Assessment*, ASCD, Alexandria, VA

Johnson, B. (Winter, 1992) "Creating Performance Assessments" *Holistic Education Review*, Brandon, VT

Kulm, G. (ed.) (1990) *Assessing Higher Order Thinking in Mathematics*, American Association for the Advancement of Science, Washington, DC

Kulm, G. (1994) *Mathematics Assessment: What Works in the Classroom* Jossey-Bass, San Francisco, CA

Linn, R., Baker, E., & Dunbar, S. (1991) "Complex, Performance-Based Assessment: Expectations and Validation Criteria," *Educational Researcher*, 20, 8 pp. 15–21 (November)

Maeroff, G. (1991) "Assessing Performance Assessment," *Phi Delta Kappan*, 73, 4; pp. 272–281 (December)

Marzano, R., Pickering, D., & McTighe, J. (1993) *Assessing Student Outcomes,* Association of Supervision & Curriculum Development, Alexandria, VA

McDonald, J. et al. (1993) *Graduation by Exhibition,* ASCD, Alexandria, VA

Mitchell, Ruth (1992) *Testing for Learning,* Free Press/Macmillan, New York, NY

Murphy, S. & Smith, M. (1991) *Writing Portfolios,* Pippin Publishing Ltd., Ontario, Canada

Neill, M. et al. (1995) *Implementing Performance Assessments,* Fairtest: The National Center for Fair & Open Testing, Cambridge, MA

Perrone, V. (ed.) (1991) *Expanding Student Assessment for Supervision and Curriculum,* ASCD, Alexandria, VA

Potter, J. (ed.) (1991) *Conversations about Assessment,* College of Education, University of Southern Maine, Gorham, ME

Rowntree, D. (1977) *Assessing Students: How Shall We Know Them?,* Nichols Publishing Co., New York, NY

Sarason, S. (1990) *The Predictable Failure of Educational Reform,* Jossey-Bass Publishers, San Francisco, CA

Selden, P. (1991) *The Teaching Portfolio,* Anker Publishing Co., Bolton, MA

Shepard, L. (1989) "Why We Need Better Assessments," *Educational Leadership,* 46, 7, pp. 4–7 (April)

Sizer, T. (1992) *Horace's School,* Houghton Mifflin, Boston, MA

Stiggins, R., Rubel, E., & Quellmalz, E. (1988) *Measuring Thinking Skills in the Classroom,* NEA Publication, Washington, DC

Stiggins, R. (1991) "Assessment Literacy," *Phi Delta Kappan,* 72, 1 pp. 534–539 (March)

Stiggins, R. (1994) *Student-Centered Classroom Assessment,* Merrill/Macmillan Publishers, New York, NY

Tierney, R., Carter, M. & Desai, L. (1991) *Portfolio Assessment in the Reading-Writing Classroom,* Christopher-Gordon Publishers, Norwood, MA

U.S. Congress, Office of Technology Assessment. *Testing in American Schools: Asking the Right Questions,* OTA–SET–519, US Government Printing Office, Washington, DC (February, 1992)

U.S. Department of Labor. (1991) *What Work Requires of Schools: A SCANS (Secretary's Commission on Achieving Necessary Skills) Report for America 2000,* US Government Printing Office, Washington, DC

Vermont Department of Education. (1989) *Vermont Writing Assessment: The Portfolio,* State of Vermont, Dept. of Education

Wiggins, G. (1993) *Student Performance: Exploring the Purpose and Limits of Testing,* Jossey-Bass, San Francisco, CA

Wiggins, G. (1991) *Toward One System of Education: Assessing to Improve,Not Merely Audit,* Education Commission of the States, Denver, CO

Wiggins, G. (1988) "Rational Numbers: Scoring and Grading that Helps Rather Than Hurts Learning," *American Educator* pp. 20–48 (Winter)

Wiggins, G. (1989) "A True Test: Toward More Authentic and Equitable Assessment," *Phi Delta Kappan.* 70, 9: 703–713 (May)

Wiggins, G. (1989) "Teaching to the (Authentic) Test," *Educational Leadership,* 46, 7, pp. 41–47 (April)

Wiggins, G. (1991) "Standards, Not Standardization: Evoking Quality Student Work," *Educational Leadership* 48, 5, pp. 18–25 (February)

Wiggins, G. (1992) "Creating Tests Worth Taking" *Educational Leadership* 49, 8, pp. 26–33 (May)

Wiggins, G. (1994) "None of the Above," *The Executive Educator,* 16, 7, pp. 14–18

Wolf, D., Bixby, J., Glen III, J., & Gardner, H. (1991) "To Use their Minds Well: Investigating New Forms of Student Assessment," in Grant, G. (ed.) (1991) *Review of Research in Education,* Washington, DC, American Educational Research Association, pp. 31–74

Wolf, D. (1987/88) "Opening Up Assessment," *Educational Leadership* 44, 4 (December/January)

Wolf, D. (1989) "Portfolio Assessment: Sampling Student Work," *Educational Leadership* 46, 7, pp. 35–39 (April)